drama STRATEGIES

New Ideas from London Drama

Dolores Deaca.

edited by
Ken Taylor

HEINEMANN EDUCATIONAL

Heinemann Educational,
a Division of Heinemann Educational Books Ltd,
Halley Court,
Jordan Hill,
Oxford OX2 8EJ

OXFORD   LONDON   EDINBURGH   MADRID
ATHENS   BOLOGNA   PARIS   MELBOURNE
SYDNEY   AUCKLAND   SINGAPORE   TOKYO
IBADAN   NAIROBI   HARARE   GABORONE
PORTSMOUTH NH (USA)

First published 1991
91 92 93 94 95 11 10 9 8 7 6 5 4 3 2

© London Drama

Cataloguing in Publication Data for this title is available from the British Library.

ISBN 0 435 18671 X

Designed by KAG Design Ltd, Basingstoke

Printed and bound by Athenaeum Press Ltd, Newcastle upon Tyne

CONTENTS

ACKNOWLEDGEMENTS

The original idea for this book grew out of the work that was being developed by Islington Drama Teachers. In 1981 we began our own self-help group which has met on a regular basis ever since to exchange ideas and lesson plans and generally to support each other. Although the constitution of the group has changed due to promotion out of the Borough the main contributors to material in this book are: Roy Baker, Judy Barnes, David Cutler-Gray, Gaynor Davies, Anita Gelb, Heather Gunn, Ann Light, Alison Royce, Barry Steer, Kenneth Taylor and David Thomas.

A further debt is owed to London Drama who have supported the work of Islington Drama Teachers from the beginning both with money and advice. Indeed it was the initial funding from London Drama which enabled us to hold our first weekend conference where the ideas for the book were originally drafted.

EDITOR'S FOREWORD

When I was asked to edit the material contained in this book I felt very humble. The material itself was excellent; tried and tested, proven to work in more than one school, and by more than one teacher. The problem was in the editorial overview I was to provide. I felt that I had little to contribute to a debate that had been illuminated so many times previously. My role was partly historical, to explain how our decisions were reached, how the material was shaped. But how could I explain the philosophy behind the work?

It occurred to me that whenever I was really stuck with my teaching I admitted this to my students. Consequently, I went into my school one Monday morning after I had wrestled with this problem for a weekend. They listened patiently to my problem, smoothed my ego and then asked the important question, `Can we do some drama now?'

Later that day I was reviewing conversations I had had with students through their drama diaries. Suddenly it was clear. There is no reason for me to say anything about our work, if it is successful the results will be sufficient. As ever the problem with the performing arts is to recall an exciting piece of practical work after the event. The very ephemeral nature of the art form which makes the creativity so challenging also makes repetition meaningless. But through our diary work we have found ways of extending and developing our practical drama experiences, so that the work can be rediscovered in other forms. It is the energy, commitment and enthusiasm that the students constantly bring to the subject that encourages me in the belief that the material is successful.

It is therefore in the hope that it will give you, the reader, more opportunities to develop your work with your own students that I offer these ideas and strategies, with the proviso that we made them work for us. It is up to you to adapt this material to your students, your situation and your style of teaching.

Kenneth Taylor

INTRODUCTION

This book divides into four sections: Organization, Lesson Structures, Techniques and Resources. While these sections can be read separately they form a coherent whole and amplify each other. The book is not meant to be read sequentially. Rather it should be interrogated for what is most useful to you. Follow up an idea and put it into practice.

The front section deals with Organization. It looks at the current position of drama, aims and objectives, readiness for learning, the Planner, planning ideas, questioning and reflection.

The middle section holds the Lesson Structures. These have been compiled by Islington Drama Teachers and are the result of regular meetings where we have shared and discussed lesson plans and practical work. The plans have been used by the group in different schools, tested and reshaped. Our intention is to offer material that has been used effectively in our classrooms and to present it openly, with our thinking, so that others can evaluate, sift through, and use what is appropriate to their own situation.

The lessons are presented in the following way:

The Advanced Organizer

Most experienced teachers find it unhelpful to carry a long list of instructions when they are teaching. We found, however, that it was useful to have a note of the key moments when the teacher held the responsibility to move the drama on. We called this an Advanced Organizer and you will see one at the start of each Lesson Structure. Really it is a simplified and condensed view of the lesson plan.

We found that the Advanced Organizer had several functions. When we were exploring new ways of working and were unsure of how to proceed, it was there as a map charting the way ahead. When we were following a familiar path but wondered what the alternatives were, it was there to suggest further opportunities. When we wanted to look ahead and take a wider perspective on the potential for the lesson when the students had introduced some new variables, it was there to remind us what the original considerations were.

General aim

Each of the Lesson Structures has a defined aim. We were working with specific groups of students in specific situations. The aim is included to indicate what we were working on with our students.

What you need

Before you go into a lesson you need to prepare any resources or materials and we felt that in a busy schedule preparation was often neglected. You can follow a lesson plan without any extra items, however we felt that time spent in preparation was doubly repaid by the interest and enthusiasm it promoted in the group.

Strategies

The strategies that are used are itemized at the top of each Lesson Structure so that you can tell at a glance which Structure gives an example of a particular strategy in action.

Action points

Each step in the lesson that called for the teacher to intervene we labelled an Action Point. The teacher has the responsibility of gauging the involvement of the group they are working with. Sometimes it will be necessary to make many interventions, sometimes fewer, but it is always the teacher's responsibility to move the lesson on. We have indicated this movement in terms of a variety of activities that help to shape and develop the drama. However, our plans cannot take account of the responses that any individual might make to the work. If you as teacher receive from a student an idea, question or role play that moves the drama forward, then it may be time to follow the students rather than the Lesson Structure. A plan is only ever a starting point. When you are confident enough it is always more exciting to explore new ground.

Each Lesson Structure follows the same format:

Left hand column

- ❏ Structure
- ❏ How you run a lesson
- ❏ A linear progression of key elements in the lesson, which tend to be Moments of teacher intervention.

Right hand column

- ❏ Commentary
- ❏ What actually happened when we used this structure
- ❏ Elaboration of the main text, sometimes offering alternatives. N.B. not every Action Point has corresponding comments.

The third section deals with Techniques such as frozen pictures, teacher in role, use of story, signing, discussion, group work, and drama related activities, video, games, using a model.

ORGANIZATION

DRAMA: THE CURRENT POSITION

For teachers who use drama the times are potentially rich and interesting. Avenues of cross-curricular development, whilst ever promising, are encouraged by now flourishing and recent legislation.

In the National Curriculum Report *English for Ages 5 to 16* (DES, 1989), drama is discussed at length and attention is drawn to its potential in promoting oral communication. Drama reveals the effectiveness of language and helps to develop an awareness of a whole range of linguistic registers, inviting students, for example, to:

❏ provide information, give instructions, and explanations;

❏ predict and plan;

❏ narrate, recount, report on a past or present experience, real or imagined;

❏ argue, discuss, defend and justify a point of view;

❏ persuade, negotiate, mediate;

❏ come to conclusions, sum up.

Reference to drama in education also appears in the *Science Non-Statutory Guidance* (DES, 1989), as a tool that will help students remember and learn more effectively; in the history draft document, as a method for giving students insight into the behaviour of people in the past and into their motivation, reactions and relationships; and in the document *Design and Technology 5-16* (DES, 1989), as both a design brief and as a way of using materials and components practically. Drama in education also has its part to play in areas designated cross-curricular by the National Curriculum, such as personal and social education, health education, careers, and coverage of gender and multi-cultural issues.

In *Drama from 5 to 16: Curriculum Matters 17* (HMSO, 1989), HMI state that drama helps to further a number of general educational purposes, and suggests that through drama students should:

❏ develop a sense of aesthetic understanding;

❏ explore the variety of human emotions;

❏ gain confidence in their own abilities, particularly to communicate verbally and non-verbally;

❏ learn to respect and, where necessary, depend upon others;

❏ develop awareness and enjoyment of the ways groups work;

❏ derive a sense of achievement from completing practical work for which they are wholly or partly responsible;

❏ evaluate their achievements as individuals and through the groups in which they work;

❏ appreciate the values and attitudes of their own and other communities.

At a time when the arguments for linking drama with English are as strong as either the arguments for linking drama with the humanities or the creative arts, there is also an urgent need to examine what is special about drama in its own right. Again the HMI document *Drama from 5 to 16: Curriculum Matters 17* (HMSO, 1989), clearly sets out the aims of learning through drama, and states that through their work students should:

❏ understand the educational, cultural and social purposes of drama;

❏ be aware of and observe dramatic conventions;

❏ use a range of dramatic forms to express ideas and feelings;

❏ practice the means of dramatic expression with fluency, vitality and enjoyment;

❏ select and shape material to achieve the maximum dramatic impact;

❏ appreciate drama in performance, both as participants and as spectators.

Through drama we recreate and examine people's actions, see how they might have come about and where they might lead. In this way, by examining human interactions, drama helps students to face intellectual, physical, social and emotional challenges. Drama in schools is a practical artistic subject. It should involve students actively and it should also be enjoyable.

Unless you know why you are teaching drama it is difficult to be clear about what an appropriate content area might be for a drama lesson. Broadly speaking there are five elements of learning possible within the context of drama in education. These areas of learning are concepts, knowledge and understanding, imagination, skills, and attitudes.

Drama in education has a special part to play in relation to students with learning difficulties. Often it is students who have most difficulty expressing themselves through writing who excel in verbal skills. Similarly, it is often those students who are disadvantaged by the core curriculum who have most to gain from drama which, if handled sensitively, is not only an excellent learning method but a vehicle that can help raise status and self esteem. As HMI state in *A Survey of the Lower Attaining Pupils Programme: The First Two Years* (DES, 1986), improvement in self-confidence, attitude and motivation have a significant influence in improving the learning potential of lower-attaining students.

Drama in education also takes advantage of mixed ability teaching and is able to set differentiated tasks. Its approach uses a cognitive-process methodology, suggesting that the learner and teacher progress together. Drama teachers do not pretend to know all the answers and do not set traps for the less able to fall into. They provide opportunities for discoveries to be made and shared.

AIMS AND OBJECTIVES IN DRAMA

In *Drama Guidelines* (London Drama and Heinemann Educational, 1976) it was stated that `the long term aim of drama teaching is to help the student to understand himself and the world he lives in.' The world moves on and while we would still subscribe to the content of this aim its language is no longer defensible. Throughout this book we are addressing all readers equally regardless of race, class, gender, ability or sexual orientation. We hope to reflect this in our writing by avoiding talking about our students as if they were all male and white (which of course they are not).

When we came to review our aims for teaching drama, Islington was involved with the Arts in Schools project. Our starting point was to consider how it was that students who had followed a school syllabus in drama for the first three years in secondary school were so ill equipped when it came to GCSE. Why was there such a discrepancy? We began by examining what we saw as the best practice within our current teaching at GCSE level, adding what we perceived as necessary to enhance the work still further, and surveying the local community groups and agencies to see what they had to offer. The result was an examination syllabus that had been built from the students upwards. The drama syllabus was accepted by the London and East Anglian Group and offered for first examination in 1990. A parallel art and design syllabus was also accepted by the board.

We feel that this syllabus offers us a way of constructing our own schemes of work within our schools, not just for the examination years but for all ages. The aims and objectives of the syllabus are set out below.

General aims

This submission is cognisant of those justifications for the place of the arts in education expressed in *The Arts in Schools* (Calouste Gulbenkian Foundation, 1982) and acknowledgement is made to that report as the basis for the general aims described below.

1.1 to play a major role in developing the full variety of human intelligence through studies in drama and theatre arts, included as an element of general education; the practice and understanding of drama and theatre arts are fundamental ways of organizing understanding of the world and call upon profound qualities of discipline and insight;

1.2 to develop the capacity for creative thought and action; the ability to innovate, initiate and make effective personal responses;

1.3 to develop the education of imagination, feeling and sensibility, and to establish an appropriate relationship between emotional and intuitive responses and those derived from intellectual and analytical processes;

1.4 to develop an ability to assess social, moral, ethical and aesthetic values through the practice and appreciation of drama and theatre arts;

1.5 to develop an understanding of cultural change and diversity; the important role in a multi-cultural society of drama and theatre arts in the expression of cultural practices and traditions, and in the evaluation and revaluation of personal cultural experience;

1.6 to develop physical and perceptual skills; to encourage the development of ideas and the ability to act upon them;

1.7 to develop the potential for further study of drama and theatre arts through the use and understanding of drama processes and practices;

1.8 to develop an understanding of the function of drama and theatre arts in relation to human communication; the recording and transmitting of verbal, visual, and spatial information; the uses and values of signs and symbols;

1.9 to develop social skills and understanding through participation in group projects and through shared experience;

1.10 to develop the ability to use drama and theatre arts in the context of other aspects of education and to develop the potential for learning through such experience.

Syllabus aims

The aims set out below are based on recognized good practice in schools and colleges, and reflect curriculum development work carried out as part of the Arts in Schools project. The syllabus framework is devised to provide maximum opportunity for centres to develop a broadly based syllabus appropriate to individual circumstances and resources as well as to select a more specialized range of study where it may be appropriate.

2.1 to develop the ability to respond creatively through drama and theatre arts to a variety of stimuli;

2.2 to develop the social awareness both of the individual and in group situations, and to relate that awareness to society in a broader sense;

2.3 to develop the ability to communicate using space, movement and language in relation to their conventional and experimental uses in the theatre; to increase the awareness of the skills, techniques and contrivances necessary to effective dramatic presentation and the ability to use them;

2.4 to use drama and theatre arts to challenge and revalue cultural assumptions, notably those concerning race, gender, class and attitudes towards disability;

2.5 to develop the ability to analyze and reflect critically; to evaluate one's own work and that of others;

2.6 to equip candidates with an awareness of techniques and strategies commonly employed in dramatic and theatrical improvization; to increase their ability to select appropriate methods of investigation;

2.7 to develop the capacity for independent study by encouraging response to direct experience, particularly the full range of theatrical performance and the planned, appropriate use of outside arts agencies such as Theatre in Education companies. It is considered that imagination develops from, and thrives upon, richness of experience, and that imaginative work is a projection of, or re-ordering of, information gained from direct experience;

2.8 to develop the use of the imagination, sensitivity and self-confidence of the individual through drama and theatre arts;

2.9 to develop the ability to create ones own presentations through an increased awareness of drama as an art form, of the means, both traditional and experimental, by which drama is communicated to an audience, and an appreciation of textual material.

READINESS FOR LEARNING

A student who is not ready to learn will not learn. This is an important consideration for often the student who is not ready to learn stops not only himself / herself from learning but the rest of the class also. Therefore the conditions for the learning to take place must be correct. The teacher must learn to read the group and pick up the signals.

Before you attempt to move the group into the drama ask yourself the following questions?

❏ Have I prepared the equipment that I need for this lesson and checked it works?
❏ Have I organized the room to create the appropriate environment for this lesson?
❏ How will I establish myself as the person responsible for the learning in this room?
❏ Will the group arrive in a positive frame of mind ready to begin?
❏ If not, what activities have I prepared to calm them down and focus their attention?
❏ How will I ensure that we can get a crisp start to the drama and engage the group with the material as soon as possible?

If you are working with a group that is familiar to you and with whom you have built a rapport you may be ready to start very quickly. If the group is new to you it may be necessary to spend a considerable amount of time establishing the rules which will govern the learning.

Be aware of how much you can negotiate with a particular class, but also of any specific school rules which must be observed. In answering the above questions it may be that you wish to involve the group. If they are co-operative, inviting them to help you organize the room may be just the right activity to prepare them for the drama. If they are an unco-operative group this may be a recipe for disaster.

Avoid rushing into the drama before the group are ready to engage with the material in the hope that the material will control the class for you. This rarely happens and often means that good material is wasted or used up without receiving adequate consideration.

Discipline can be maintained from within the drama so long as the students know what is expected outside the drama. A teacher who meets a group for the first time and then works immediately in role starts at a disadvantage. The group need to be aware of the baseline.

Once you have successfully established the level of participation, concentration, motivation, and commitment that you expect from the group it will be easier in future to insist that you get it. From the students' point of view, work within the arts is 'harder' than work within the other school subject areas because it demands constant self-control and the ability to think and behave creatively. They are responsible for much of what happens within the lesson and they must learn not only to feel this responsibility but to respond positively to it. They are part of a group and must exercise the appropriate social control to ensure that the group dynamic remains a healthy one.

The teacher has the final responsibility for managing the interactions that take place within the classroom. If this is undertaken with a positive attitude from the beginning and if the students are invited to participate in the decisions being made then the atmosphere will remain firm but friendly. Surprisingly, students often prefer those teachers who retain tight control over their classes to those who appear more liberal. Generally students respond favourably to those teachers who can organize positive experiences, remain ruthlessly fair, and who can encourage an active involvement in the work.

Just as a student not ready to learn will not learn, a student not ready to participate within the art form cannot be made to. It is a nonsense to imagine the strict drama teacher standing over the recalcitrant child demanding he / she works in role now! Therefore a readiness and a willingness to engage in the art form are as necessary as the willingness to learn.

This juggling act is not an easy one but it is one that can be learned and refined. The effort is always rewarded with a secure platform from which to build enjoyable drama lessons.

THE PLANNER

On the next page is a planning chart. We have found it useful as a device to aid thinking when devising lesson structures.

We chose ten key areas to consider when planning a lesson:

- ❏ teacher in role
- ❏ discussion
- ❏ pair work
- ❏ frozen picture
- ❏ story
- ❏ group work
- ❏ presentation
- ❏ second teacher in role
- ❏ stimuli
- ❏ drama related activities.

Each of these areas is dealt with in the Techniques section after the Lesson Structures. There are obviously additional areas that could be included, which is why we left a space marked `?'

The central bubble is for the learning area, idea, theme, topic or concept that initiates the planning. We suggest that the central bubble can be developed through each of the areas. The teacher's own good practice will dictate which is finally chosen.

This chart can be used on its own or in conjunction with the plans set out in this book. For an example see the following pages.

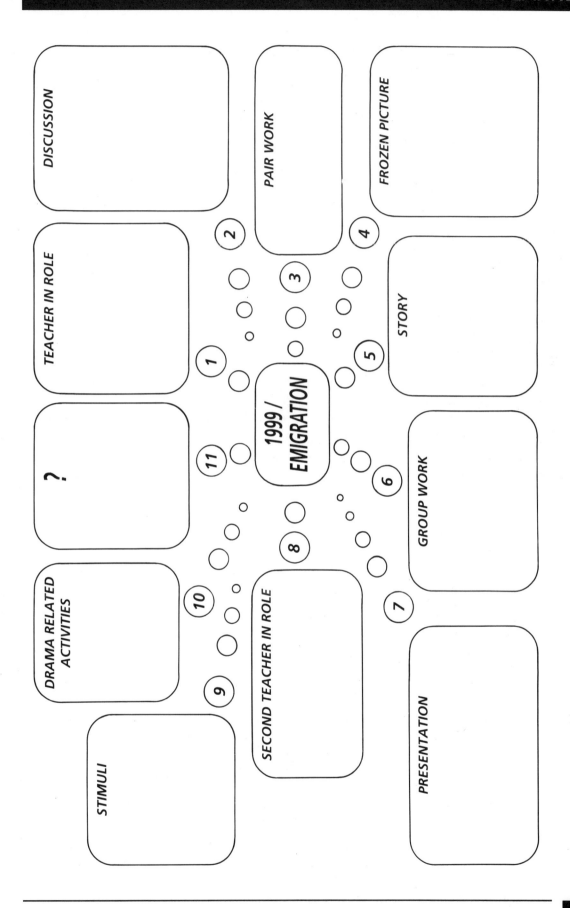

DISCUSSION

PAIR WORK

FROZEN PICTURE

TEACHER IN ROLE

STORY

?

GROUP WORK

DRAMA RELATED ACTIVITIES

SECOND TEACHER IN ROLE

PRESENTATION

STIMULI

1999 / EMIGRATION

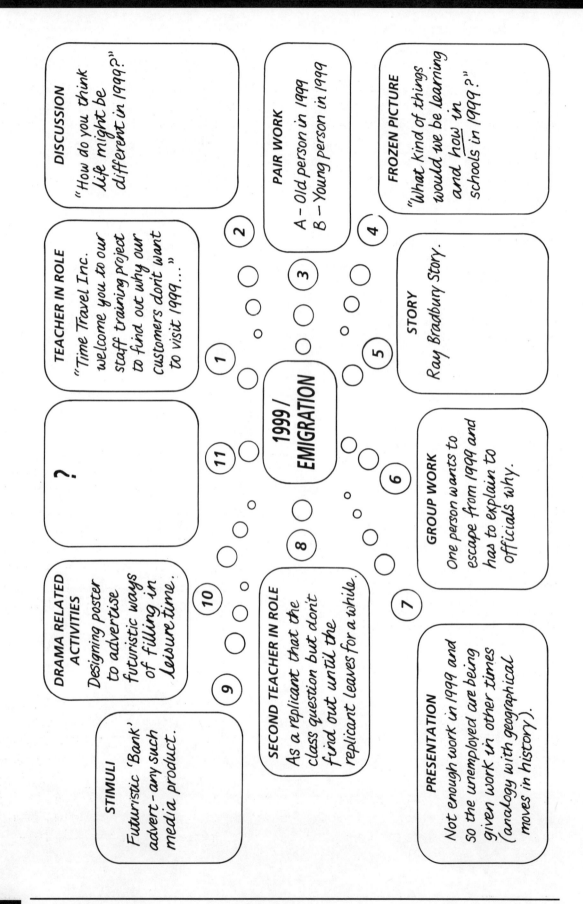

DISCUSSION

"How do you think life might be different in 1999?"

PAIR WORK

A – Old person in 1999
B – Young person in 1999

FROZEN PICTURE

"What kind of things would we be learning and how in schools in 1999?"

TEACHER IN ROLE

"Time Travel Inc. welcome you to our staff training project to find out why our customers don't want to visit 1999..."

STORY

Ray Bradbury Story.

?

1999 / EMIGRATION

GROUP WORK

One person wants to escape from 1999 and has to explain to officials why.

DRAMA RELATED ACTIVITIES

Designing poster to advertise futuristic ways of filling in leisure time.

SECOND TEACHER IN ROLE

As a replicant that the class question but don't find out until the replicant leaves for a while.

PRESENTATION

Not enough work in 1999 and so the unemployed are being given work in other times (analogy with geographical moves in history).

STIMULI

Futuristic 'Bank' advert – any such media product.

1 2 3 4 5 6 7 8 9 10 11

PLANNING IDEAS

When planning work it is important to offer as much variety as possible so that your delivery of the material stays fresh and the interest level of the students remains high. As well as using the Planner to vary your starting points for each particular lesson it is worth having a long-term view which reflects a variety of input. As an aid to planning and certainly as an aid to more interesting lessons we suggest that each term you offer a variety of:

- ❏ aims and objectives
- ❏ content
- ❏ assessment
- ❏ learning areas
- ❏ resources
- ❏ skills tested
- ❏ stimuli or starting points
- ❏ ways of working
- ❏ syllabus relevance

To help with your planning we have used the above headings to list some ideas which we have found successful.

Aims and objectives

Rather than assume that by carrying on with your lessons in the normal way you are delivering your agreed aims, work at them specifically. Look at your GCSE syllabus or departmental aims. Divide up these aims over a period of time so that for a specific class for a specific period of time you can concentrate on a specific aim. You may spend four weeks with a first year group focusing on encouraging co-operative behaviour. Share this focus on aims and objectives, explain to them what they need to do to achieve the goal and build in an opportunity at some point to assess how successful you have been. Not only will this allow you to offer a variety of aims and objectives throughout the year it will improve your delivery of them.

Content

Everyone tires of repetition, so it is important to vary the content area of the drama as much as possible. For a teacher the search for suitable material for a drama lesson is a constant one, so share the load. Talk with people, find out what they are interested in. Ask colleagues what areas they are currently teaching and what interests them about this. Encourage students to tell you when they have been fascinated, appalled, shocked or amused by something. Suggest that they could bring in interesting photographs or news stories and reward them for their effort. Of course, the best reward is to use their material. Finding content is a responsibility, but, like most other things in drama, it is one that can be shared.

Assessment

In order for there to be progression in the drama work a variety of assessment objectives should be considered over a period of time. It is easier to target a few individuals each lesson, say five, rather than assess the whole class. Alternatively, you could look at everyone but only consider very few assessment objectives. Explain to your group which assessment objectives are currently under consideration and explain what they have learnt and what they must show to achieve well on these criteria. It is an obvious point that children perform better when they know what they are expected to achieve.

It is also important to be aware of the purpose of the assessment. There are four main types of assessment:

❏ formative - which takes place during the Drama process, ideally involves the children and attempts to diagnose progress and development;
❏ summative - which records the achievement of learners over a period of time and is completed at the end of a block of work;
❏ diagnostic - which takes place when there is a perceived problem with either the Drama work or the learner's ability to participate and a remedy is sought;
❏ evaluative - which attempts to reflect on the quality of the engagement in the process.

Learning areas

The learning areas that are possible in drama are infinite, although they tend to fall into a particular type. To a certain extent the learning areas that are likely to occur will depend upon your teaching style. However, it is possible to consider other areas and have short as well as long term aims. If you tend to focus on communication and social skills introduce some theatre arts skills. If you are primarily skills based introduce some lessons that have historical sources and offer the opportunity to gain knowledge. If the learning is often personal introduce broad themes and look at the universal implications. If your learning areas tend to occur only within the drama consider what other activities you could set up in school or at home that would support and develop the work.

Resources

Drama lessons can often be 'poor' in terms of resources in a way that maths or English lessons are not. What resources are there available in your school that you are not regularly taking advantage of? For example, a block loan of books from the school or local library on the current topic; a portable computer with printer to produce customized documents, letters or drawings for a particular piece of drama; another teacher to be used in role; photocopies of news items or photographs. A box full of unwanted objects and material found from around the school may be of no use to anyone in particular, but ideal to start an imaginative journey into drama.

Skills tested

In order to analyze the progress that your teaching is prompting in the students it will be necessary at certain times to organize some kind of evaluative session. On these occasions take the opportunity to look for different skills. There may well be times when you wish to encourage and reward research just as much as skill at improvisation. Look at what students are good at and seek to develop this, rather than impose a structure from outside. Take the opportunity to celebrate individual success. If you have a bilingual learner in the group who has the confidence to use both languages in the drama, find opportunities for this to be recognized.

Stimuli or starting points

As was said of content above, repetition is tedious. Classes quickly recognize a pattern and may slip into routine and unthinking response if the work becomes boring and predictable. Because you enjoy working in role with your group and are convinced it immediately moves the drama into a higher gear it does not mean that the group will not see this as an expected pattern and respond accordingly, losing the freshness and spontaneity to which you originally responded. With a little thought numerous different starting points can be uncovered, even for the same material. For example, we have found each of the following to be appropriate starting points:

- ❏ Analogy
- ❏ Anecdote
- ❏ Ceremony
- ❏ Collection of objects - handbag containing personal possessions, etc.
- ❏ Costume
- ❏ Diaries, letters, journals, messages
- ❏ Discussion
- ❏ Drama related activities
- ❏ File / information
- ❏ Forum theatre
- ❏ Frozen photograph
- ❏ Game
- ❏ Giving witness
- ❏ Horoscope
- ❏ Hot-seating
- ❏ Interviews / interrogations
- ❏ Meeting
- ❏ Mime
- ❏ Narration
- ❏ Newspapers
- ❏ Obituary - the outline of someone's life, could also use
      Concise Dictionary of National Biography
- ❏ Overheard conversations
    - ○ misheard / mistaken
    - ○ about the hearer
    - ○ real
- ❏ Photographs or pictures
- ❏ Photoplay / photostory
- ❏ Piece of movement
- ❏ Sound and movement sandwich
- ❏ Crossing the room in various ways, etc.
- ❏ Piece of music

- ❏ Piece of script
- ❏ Piece of video
- ❏ Students in role
- ❏ Planning an environment
- ❏ Poem
- ❏ Presentation
- ❏ Problem page letter
- ❏ Props
- ❏ Re-enactment
- ❏ Records or sound tapes
- ❏ Ritual
- ❏ Shadow play
- ❏ Simulation
- ❏ Slides
- ❏ Small group playmaking
- ❏ Story
- ❏ Teacher in role
- ❏ Teacher in role - monologue
- ❏ TV commercials
- ❏ Unbelievable stories
- ❏ What do you want to do a play about?

Ways of working

The following ways of working arise from our work on the Mode II GCSE Drama and Theatre Arts syllabus. We feel, however, these hold true across the age range.

Project based thematic enquiry and response

This refers to a scheme of work which sets out to explore a particular topic. Although maximum opportunity is given to develop the work in a variety of ways, it is still constrained by an established theme. For example, a scheme of work might look at problems related to drug abuse. Consideration would need to be given to the way in which the topic is introduced, research would be conducted to establish material which is then used as the basis for a programme of improvisation. By selecting work generated in this way, a presentation could be devised.

Sequential development

This refers to a scheme of work planned on a structured system which aims at an accumulation of specific skills, knowledge and understanding over a fixed period of time. For example, a scheme of work might set out to develop the ability to use the technique of still image or depiction. It may begin with work requiring a relatively descriptive or naturalistic use of the technique, such as constructing a 'photograph' imagined to have been taken on a particular occasion, progress to using the technique to express individual abstract ideas or emotions, such as constructing a depiction which expresses 'jealousy', then apply the technique to the task of expressing a more complex series of concepts, such as constructing a series of tableaux to represent Shakespeare's 'Seven Ages of Man' speech.

Expressive response

This refers to the unrestricted exploration and development of ideas and feelings through appropriate choice of drama and theatre arts practices. This way of working would usually be preceded by exposure to a particular stimulus or perhaps a current event of particular relevance or significance to the candidates.

For example, the teacher may choose from a wide range of stimuli: photographs, poems, stories, music, script extracts. The direction of the work would be dictated by the candidates' response and interest, with the teacher shaping and facilitating through negotiation.

Structured discussion, critical appraisal and analysis

This refers to the formulation and articulation of value judgements about drama and theatre arts. For example, discussion may often take place following the completion of a particular unit of work in order to evaluate the work. This could be a whole group discussion, or between individual candidates, or between an individual candidate and the teacher. Discussion may also take place in a formative way, as a means of shaping the drama.

Problem solving and restricted exploration

This refers to specific task-setting closely related to established drama and theatre arts theory and practice wherein candidates might be required to consider a range of ideas and solutions and select appropriate media. For example, the candidates may see some examples, live or video recorded, of Theatre in Education companies working with the Primary age range. Particular techniques will be analyzed and reflected upon with the help of the teacher, or, if possible, the company concerned. The candidates may then be set the problem-solving brief of preparing a programme on road safety to be presented at a local 'feeder' primary school. The resulting programme may be presented by arrangement with a local school, and work in progress as well as the end 'product' could be evaluated and recorded by the candidates.

Research, analysis, observation and recording

This refers to methods of approach, appropriate technical skills, and the development of an ability to use information retrieval and reference systems. For example, as part of a series of improvisations on the theme of `prejudice' candidates might be asked to look through a selection of newspapers and select examples of what they consider to be racist reporting. From their selection they may be asked if it is possible to delineate a set of criteria for determining the language of institutionalized racism. This language study may then further resource explorative work in improvisation or preparation for presentation.

Syllabus relevance

When you look at a syllabus you will find that it is quite easy to break it down into small parts. It is then possible to consider what needs to be taught to cover this or that area of the syllabus. This in itself may give you inspiration in devising material for your classroom.

QUESTIONING

Questioning is one of the most important skills that a teacher using drama can develop. With acknowledgement to Roma Burgess and Pamela Gaudry as well as David Sheppard we have developed an analysis of questions that can be asked both from within the drama and from outside.

There are three areas that need careful examination:

❏ facts clearly stated by the drama
❏ things inferred by the action
❏ what we do not yet know.

One way we have found that gets this idea across to the students is to stop the drama and ask them in reference to the play as it has occurred so far what they can guess and what they know. If their responses are publicly recorded then the group begins to build a consensus which will aid further development of the drama. In order for this to be successful an agreement must be sought early on so that we can believe what the characters tell us.

Always be aware of whether you need to ask an open or closed question. There will be occasions when you need a yes or no answer from the group, but if you want them to take control themselves it may be better to ask open questions. For example:

Open
❏ How would you like the play to develop?
❏ How did your character affect the outcome of the play?
❏ As the thief, how did you feel when the lights were turned on and the old couple came into the room?

Closed
❏ Did you enjoy that work?
❏ Would you play that character again?
❏ As the thief, were you pleased when you found the window open?

The teacher should be aware of the range of questions that are available to be asked and also encourage the group to ask different types of question. Here is a list of types of question with examples:

Analysis
Who were you in the play?

Hypothesis
If a bomb dropped on the youth club how would you have responded?

Evaluation
What has this taught you about the nature of bureaucracy? Does this give you any idea?

Synthesis
How will your life be different now that they have built a road through the forest?

Analogy
Can you think of other situations where this might happen? Give me an example?

Deduction
Why do you think the King wants a road?

Form
When John was hiding from Angela who had just come into the room and was looking around, what did this tell us about the play?

There may be occasions when the group need more help or you particularly wish to push them in a certain direction. In this case you may need to use a branching question. For example:

Would you like to see what happens to the customs officer or to the smuggler?

Would you like to make things more difficult for the suspects or easier?

A branching question usually restricts choice to two alternatives. The alternatives are chosen by the teacher so in a sense this is a very closed question, but it can lead on to more open questions.

QUESTIONING

Remember there are a variety of ways that you can use questioning. It can help you:

- ❑ check on the response from the group
- ❑ deepen their response
- ❑ develop the work
- ❑ find out what interests them
- ❑ define the learning area
- ❑ build belief in the work
- ❑ evaluate / assess the work.

REFLECTION

Although within these structures we have suggested how reflection might take place at the end of each section opportunities for reflection can be built in at any point in the lesson and should not always be left as something tacked on at the end. Handled well, reflection will enable the participants to clarify their thoughts about the work in progress and this in turn will promote greater depth in the work.

It is also important to note that when allowing time for students to reflect it is also possible to allow time for the teacher to gather their thoughts and consider their next strategy.

Opportunities for reflection can be achieved most easily when the students are placed at a distance from the immediate work. This may be done with them either in or out of role. For example, in the structure *Drugs* you could stop the drama at the point just before the drug dealers and the undercover members of the Drug Squad meet. In each case they could then be invited to play the parents of these characters talking to neighbours about what their children did on this particular evening. In this way you are asking the students to comment as another character upon what they are actually doing. Although this is in role it is inviting comment and reflection on the situation.

Interestingly this is inviting the group to invent forward rather than think back at past events. An example of an out of role opportunity for reflection at the same moment might be to stop the drama at the same point and ask them all to prepare a written or tape recorded news item of the meeting that night as it might appear if a journalist had witnessed the events. Here they are being asked to give an objective account of events not the position from the point of view of the character they are playing. Again they are being asked to create a future for the play that has not yet been played out, therefore whatever is created cannot be 'wrong'. It is merely their version of events.

There are a number of ways that we have attempted to build in moments of reflection:

❏ distance in time
❏ distance in space
❏ distance through role
❏ frozen picture - of a key moment
❏ frozen picture - to symbolize an abstraction of feeling
❏ sequence of frozen pictures - like a cartoon strip
❏ frozen picture into key words, sound, music
❏ frozen picture into movement, dance
❏ hot-seating a character; interviews; chat shows

- ❏ monologue, soliloquy - aloud or silent
- ❏ voice-over depiction; conscience; thoughts *vs* spoken words
- ❏ one generation to another; second generation to another
- ❏ dreams, nightmares, ghosts
- ❏ symbolic objects - the old box in the loft, photograph, bunch of keys
- ❏ out of practical into the written form - diaries, journals, letters

If opportunities for reflection are offered and taken up throughout the lesson then the tired old structure of giving a stimulus, working in groups and then presenting your work to the rest of the class can be avoided. Such a form of presentation will, without doubt, still be desirable at times. However, we have found that by varying the structure of a lesson, groups can be given other opportunities to express their creativity and weaned from preparing and showing in every lesson.

There are many different ways of organizing the presentation part of the lesson so that you can begin to break down this cycle:

- ❏ Do not allow them to present the work they have prepared but tell them to improvise the scene that continues from where theirs finished!
- ❏ Use the work the group has prepared in groups as character work and develop a whole group scene where these characters come together.
- ❏ Frozen picture and questioning - for example, freeze one moment from their play that shows tension, or is a particularly striking visual image.
- ❏ Watch part of their presentation then ask them to improvise what happened five minutes before / after the scene they have just created.
- ❏ Each group could work on different scenes which build toward a whole - for example, a day in the life of one character where each group takes a different time of day.
- ❏ What if? - use their work in a different way, suppose it was police evidence on video, etc.
- ❏ Teacher in role could enter the work as it is presented to challenge and change the scene from inside.
- ❏ Offer a frame for the audience as they watch the scene - for example, doctors viewing what led to the accident and commenting upon it.

ADVANCED ORGANIZER - DRUGS

Possible Developments

?

STIMULUS
Improvised Scene

FLASHBACK
What were the
dealers / officers doing
before this scene?

GROUP WORK
Based on above

**INTEREST
COMING FROM THE
GROUP**

WHOLE GROUP & TEACHER
Press conference

GROUP WORK
Drug Dealers
Drug Squad

PAIR WORK
Dealer / Squad

GROUP WORK
Telling

MODEL
Mimed meeting
Drug Ring & Strangers

GROUP WORK
One wants to leave

WHOLE GROUP & TEACHER
Press conference

REFLECTION
Questioning

THROUGH LINE LOGIC

DRUGS

General aims

To develop awareness and knowledge of the dangers associated with drugs and also the exploitation of young people through the drug industry.

What you need

Optional - drug information leaflets available from doctors' surgeries and hospitals.
See also Resources 1, 5 and 12 pages 128, 131 and 138.

Strategies

Teacher in role, group work, pair work, signing, mime, using a model, verbal and non-verbal language work.

ACTION POINTS

Stimulus

❑ Improvise a scene at the front for the rest of the group to watch. TIR as the customs' officer. Two volunteers as drug dealers.

❑ Play out the scene. The dealers are bringing drugs in through customs.

❑ Afterwards comment on the effectiveness of the scene, discuss things like tension and suspense. How might they develop this scene?

❑ Replay the scene using suggestions from the group to develop tension and suspense. Also consider how the space is used.

❑ Ask the question, `As a customs' officer who has done this work for some time what would you be looking for?'

❑ Take their suggestions and if they do not raise it, which is unlikely, discuss body language. These ideas will help the volunteers get the scene `right'.

This lesson was devised to challenge a group of students who had an idealized idea of drug taking. They were interested in `playing' junkies but the learning contract made with the class was that at the start they were in role as drug dealers who were not users. This distancing was deliberate, not only to protect the students (some of whom may well know more about drugs than others), but also to enhance the possibilities for the drama.

To ensure that the students are engaged in this activity they must feel that it is a tense moment. The TIR can be very suspicious and almost catch the drug dealers, but then lets them pass through.

GROUP WORK

❏ In groups they generate their own scenes based on the one observed. Their objective is to create a `customs' scene with tension in it.

Having watched a scene unfold in this way most students are capable of developing their own work. In our lessons we found that this was an excellent way to practice and develop specific skills. In this case developing the use of tension within a scene and shaping their own work.

WHOLE GROUP WITH TEACHER IN ROLE

❏ TIR as police spokesperson giving a press conference. The police have failed to locate the drug dealers but they must not allow the press to get hold of this information.
They are concerned to keep up the appearance of an efficient police force.

❏ Students in role as members of the press. The press strongly suspect that a huge amount of heroin has entered the country and want to get the police to admit their failure.

Teacher role play allows a lot of information to be given which will enhance future work: for example, possible corruption in the police force, responsibility of the press to police and public, etc. Signing will be important here. Similarly setting mode and language register through example. In this scene we wanted a formal meeting and we worked for this by speaking in role in a heightened way and referring to the normal procedure at a press conference. By careful use of expression and body language the teacher can demonstrate that what is said is not the whole truth.

DRUGS

GROUP WORK

❏ Split the class in half and within each large group organize them into groups of about five. To one half explain:

You are drug dealers. One of you must become the leader of the drug ring who knows that the police are on to them. Members of the ring must therefore get rid of the heroin as quickly as possible but also be very careful as to whom they deal with.

❏ To the other half explain:
You are members of the Drug Squad. One of you must be the Chief Inspector whose task is to get to the top people in the drug ring. The small dealers are no good. The Drug Squad therefore go under-cover, attempt to make deals and become `dealers' themselves.

Act out the scenes of the leaders warning their groups and planning strategies of how to proceed.

It is important that the teacher takes part in this group work as much of the development of this particular drama needs teacher information from within the drama. If the teacher visits each group in role it is possible not only to help build the play but also through questioning in role to build belief and a strong second dimension or attitude which in turn will help create tension.

It may further help the work if materials are brought in which give further background to the drama. For example, there are many leaflets that point out the dangers of drug taking. These often list symptoms and describe how a person may be affected in appearance and mood.

PAIR WORK

The pairs should consist of one from each `half' of the class. Label these pairs A and B, then explain:
A = drug dealer in usual meeting place waiting for contact.
B = Drug Squad undercover agent approaches to make deal.
The pairs improvise this encounter.

The second dimension or attitude for these roles is informed by the previous group work.

GROUP WORK

- ❏ In the same groups of about five, drug dealers and members of the Drug Squad regroup and share their experiences 'out in the field'. This should be done in role.
- ❏ In shaping this work encourage the group to consider the setting, for example, where does their meeting take place? Also consider atmosphere, are they going to be afraid that they will be discovered or are they confident that they are secure? It may be an interesting comparison to compare how the two groups approach this.

This can be repeated with various new tensions in-built in order to build belief. For example, one member of the dealers could say that they have made contact with a new trader who knows one of the dealers. The person claimed to be known has never heard of the new contact. Then back to pair work to try to catch out the new contact. (All the time with the over-riding tension of 'we must get rid of this heroin as soon as possible!') Various new tensions can be introduced in order to build appropriate belief.

MODEL

- ❏ TIR and volunteers role play a demonstration while students watch. This is a mimed meeting between leaders of the drug ring and a stranger and takes place on a park bench. The episode is overseen by one of the drug ring who can tell that they are making some kind of deal. Unfortunately what is said cannot be made out.

An action point to build distrust between members of the drug ring. This could be set up as a piece of 'video tape' made by a police surveillance team, either watched by the police or which has fallen into the hands of the dealers. In any case it is 'evidence'. We encouraged those watching to make their own interpretations of what was happening and even to suggest dialogue. It may be that the group need time to attempt their own reconstruction.

Group members at this point may begin to demand answers of their leader. This also works very well on the level of 'Well, we've come this far and we can't opt out now.'

GROUP WORK

❏ In the same groups of about five as drug dealers and members of the Drug Squad they act out the following scenes.

❏ Drug dealers:
One of the drug dealers wants to leave the group. He / she has been `scared off' and no longer want any part of the operation. The others are not sure whether they can trust him / her.

❏ Drug Squad:
One member of the Drug Squad is actually a drug user who is becoming more dependant on drugs and hence is a weak link in the force. He is found in the locker room asleep after having almost blown a raid by lack of concentration the previous night.

This action point is beginning to approach the area that the students are really interested in, that is, the drug users! By now the students should have built enough belief and be approaching the subject in the right frame of mind. This is also the point at which we are approaching the intended aim of the topic. At this stage the students may also consider a raid. A possible way of doing this is through using freeze frame where the drug squad find their former officer in a terrible state through use of drugs. Possible ways of building tension might be that one of the police officers has a sister who has died of a drug overdose etc.

WHOLE GROUP WITH TEACHER IN ROLE

❏ TIR as police spokesperson giving a press conference. The police have failed but must not allow the press to get hold of this information. Concerned to keep up appearances of an efficient police force.

❏ SIR as members of the press. The press strongly suspect that a huge amount of heroin has entered the country and want to get the police to admit their failure.

The teacher should ensure by the way he / she plays the police spokesperson that the press are in a much stronger position now. With careful management many large issues can be raised in this forum. For example, access to information, the right of the press to report the facts, withholding information `in the best interest of the public'.

REFLECTION

Questioning by the teacher of the group out of role. There is new information now for this confrontation between the police and the press. How does it change the scene?

Having played the press conference scene at the beginning it is interesting to compare the two scenes. Invite the students to say how they think it is different and why this should be. It may have become necessary earlier in the work to refer to leaflets that have been produced about drugs and drug taking. Whether this is the case or not it would be useful here to refer to such materials and to agencies where advice can be sought.

DEVELOPMENT

You may care to consider the following:
❏ Make a list of legal and illegal drugs. Why are some legal and others not?
❏ Watch the BBC Scene programme *Too Nice By Half* which focuses on two school boys who become involved with drugs.
❏ Design a warning commercial to campaign against drugs. This could be videoed or recorded.
❏ Find a map which takes you to the producer of the drugs. In fact this is a peasant farmer who gets more for this particular crop than any other but is still very poor. How can you persuade him / her to change the crop he / she grows?

Possible Developments

?

STIMULUS
Newspaper Headline

WHOLE GROUP & TEACHER
Warden / Senior Warder
& Inmates

GROUP WORK
What had they done to
deserve this ?

WHOLE GROUP & TEACHER
Warden / Senior Warder
& Inmates

**INTEREST
COMING FROM THE
GROUP**

GROUP WORK
The disappearance

WHOLE GROUP & TEACHER
Warden / Senior Warder
'Chose two...'

SMALL GROUPS
defend

WHOLE GROUP & TEACHER
Warden angry

VIDEO
Live or recorded

WHOLE GROUP & TEACHER
Warden & Journalists

FROZEN PICTURE
What's happening ?

SMALL GROUPS
Tactics

GROUP WORK
Confrontation

WHOLE GROUP & TEACHER
Warden sees video

DISCUSSION

THROUGH LINE LOGIC

HILLSIDE UNIT

General aims

To stimulate thought on the use of duplicity and deceit. To make the class aware of irony as a dramatic form.

What you need

Video recorder and camera (optional). Two teachers for at least one session. Newspaper headline made up from newspapers. See Resources 2, 4 and 7 pages 128, 130 and 133.

Strategies

Discussion, second teacher in role, signing, frozen pictures, role within a role, group work, video.

ACTION POINTS

Stimulus

Newspaper headline displayed, `Drama Group Sent to Secure Unit.' Discussion of what this might mean.

This lesson was inspired by a colleague who had been having problems within their tutor group concerning the theft of small items. Although the items were of little value the distress caused was great. The lesson was devised to encourage the group to reconsider its actions more carefully. It was not devised merely to portray punishment as the answer for all wrongdoing, but to encourage the group to consider justice and personal responsibility.

Work can precede this unit on why a group should be sent to a secure unit (that is, areas of conflict in society for young people), which would build belief in role and characterization.

HILLSIDE UNIT

WHOLE GROUP WITH TEACHER IN ROLE

- ❏ TIR 1 as the warden welcoming new inmates - pleasantly detailing limited infringements of freedom.
- ❏ TIR 2 as senior warder gives a different view through body language and signing.
- ❏ SIR as inmates.

Introduction of theme. Do not trust what you see or hear. Students encouraged to question by TIR 2's obvious disbelief. What is said is belied by the physical gestures and expression. This is the first point where they should be encouraged to think for themselves within the drama and exercise personal responsibility.

WHOLE GROUP WITH TEACHER IN ROLE

TIR 1 as warden leaves SIR to ask TIR 2 as senior warder questions. The truth comes out about the conditions. It is further revealed that people are disappearing.

Students get their first opportunity to try out what they have observed in role. Work could include out-of-role discussion of the situation and lead into group work, or actor / thinker strategy to develop this.

GROUP WORK

In groups develop a scene showing how the inmates might disappear.

Encourage the group to work in one style. If they are being naturalistic tell them this. If they prefer comedy then explore this first.

WHOLE GROUP WITH TEACHER IN ROLE

- ❏ TIR 2 as senior warder warns inmates that the warden is planning to make two people disappear.
- ❏ TIR 1 as warden chooses two inmates 'to come into my office in half an hour.'

Ideas from this direct the rest of the lesson.

SMALL GROUPS

Group is set task of defending the two chosen.

This can be approached as whole group work in role, if group has cohered, or as group work.

WHOLE GROUP WITH TEACHER IN ROLE

The group meet the warden who is angry that the two inmates have not reported to his / her office yet. They voice their objections. The warder is very angry and high handed. He / she may need to reduce their existing privileges if they do not co-operate.

This role will be helped if the TIR 2 reacts in role attempting to warn the inmates not to provoke the warden. They have a difficult decision to make, what is their responsibility in this situation?

WHOLE GROUP WITH TEACHER IN ROLE

TIR 1 as warden and SIR as newspaper / investigative team with a video that they have been sent anonymously. It shows the warden and the senior warder talking about the goings on at the unit. Warden is not eager to see the video now but reluctantly agrees to meet the team later. This is a very brief scene.

Change of tack to offer a distancing effect to examine the material more closely and to remove the pressure on the two inmates who have not reported to the warden. Some students have trouble disassociating themselves from the previous role and the knowledge gained. This makes the drama more objective - moving from direct involvement to a wider perspective. A discussion of newspaper ethics / angles might deepen this approach. Room here to look at duplicity of investigators' moral / financial motivation. In whose interest does this happen? The group and the teacher can plan together what should appear on the video and it can be recorded in advance or acted live 'as if' it were a piece of video - that is, able to be replayed, stopped and started. We found that a short piece of video which was very ambiguous, full of suggestive nods and winks, as if the people in the video were concerned they might be overheard, worked best. This also leaves open the possibility that things are perfectly innocent within the unit and the warden has been set up. It is important that the video shows the warders and not the inmates, it is not an excuse to show violence or brutality.

SMALL GROUPS

Groups of investigators plan their tactics for the interview of the warden. What will be their best approach to get at the truth? Who shall they pretend to be? They know what is on the video (this can be agreed in advance), the question is how will the warden react when he / she sees it.

It is stressed that a direct approach will not get information. Subtlety and deceit may be needed.

WHOLE GROUP WITH TEACHER IN ROLE

TIR 1 as warden meets the investigators outside the room where they are to watch the video. he / she is nervous and clearly stalling for time. Perhaps the key cannot be found or the door is difficult to open.

This scene gives the groups something definite to work from. It should relate to ideas they have provided.

VIDEO

They watch the video which has caused the investigators concern (and which the investigators have already seen). Of course, their focus is not the video but how the warden will respond to what he / she sees.

If only one teacher is available for subsequent sessions this could be an actual video. Otherwise this can be acted, perhaps with a student 'controlling the machine'. The similarity with the play scene in *Hamlet* is deliberate as it may serve as a jumping off point to other work, for instance, 'shall we look at how a playwright tackled exactly the same situation that we used in our play?'

FROZEN PICTURE

In groups they have two minutes to create their own still picture of what is happening at the unit. They should think of this as a photograph for the newspaper.

This reinforces the investigators' ideas of what they are working on, while allowing little re-identification with first role as inmates. It also stops the previous scene from developing too quickly before the students have had time to consider the implications.

GROUP WORK

Show confrontation between the warden and the investigators in disguise. Do they get a confession or information?

A role within a role. As well as discussing the effectiveness of strategy to get information, morality, etc., at another level a discussion on role-playing techniques is possible. The students handle the double role play in different ways - they should be made aware of the complexity of their achievement.

DISCUSSION

On things not being what they seem.

DEVELOPMENT

You may care to consider the following:
- ❏ What would the entries in the diary of one of the inmates kept in solitary confinement look like?
- ❏ Write the newspaper story.
- ❏ What happens to the inmates after they leave the unit? Do they gain fame or notoriety?

- ❏ What power do you believe fiction has? Would a scene of someone's guilt be sufficient to cause them to confess? Make connections to *Hamlet*.
- ❏ How do the public respond when the real story is told?

THROUGH LINE LOGIC

Possible Developments ← **?**

STIMULUS
Editor tells the story

STOP THE DRAMA
Check the understanding

MODEL
Planning an interview

PAIR WORK
Journalist / Photographer
Planning interview

WHOLE GROUP & TEACHER
Editor calls for
report back

PAIR WORK
Journalist / Photographer
Rehearse interview

PAIR WORK FROZEN PICTURE
Journalist / Photographer
rehearse photograph

WHOLE GROUP & TEACHER
Discussion about Maria

WHOLE GROUP & TEACHER
Maria interviewed

WHOLE GROUP & TEACHER
Editor asks for a
report back

GROUP WORK
Maria's family The Day
of the Arrest

**INTEREST
COMING FROM THE
GROUP**

WHOLE GROUP & TEACHER
Story will not
be printed

NARRATION

WHOLE GROUP & TEACHER
Now print

REFLECTION

THE STORY OF MARIA

General aims

To introduce the idea of censorship and notions of trust, distrust, loyalty, betrayal.

What you need

A story - see below. Optional - clipboards, paper, pens. See also Resources 3, 16 and 17 pages 129 and 142.

Strategies

Teacher in role - second in command, pair work, story and narrative, interviews, frozen pictures, using a model.

ACTION POINTS

Stimulus

TIR as newspaper editor tells the story of Maria to the class who are in role as journalists eager to get an article.

The teacher can use their own story for this work or follow the outline of the story we used.

TIR says, 'The story is a tip-off, an exclusive and under wraps. Five years ago the paper did an article on Maria's trial. At the time we printed this ...'

`... Maria Gonzalez was today sentenced to seven years in prison for a crime she still denies committing. The judge in passing sentence called her a cold, calculating person capable of anything and he consequently resolved to use the full power of the law to deter her and others like her from such insane acts in the future. Her mother, who was in the courtroom, kept shouting out, `There must be some mistake.' '

Often in the past drama lessons have concerned themselves with trust exercises and establishing positive group feelings. While this has its place within a school drama lesson, in the real world it would be a mistake to trust everyone. An ability to discriminate or criticise may be preferable. Students should sometimes exercise a healthy distrust, for example if they met a stranger who offered them sweets.

The original newspaper story can be created prior to the lesson or as a new part of the lesson using the students' ideas. One way we found successful was to get another class to produce the original version of the story in a mocked-up newspaper front page.

If the details of the story are left vague you can then encourage the group to help invent the drama. They may even need to do some research. Where might an 18-year-old that has left home live? Why might she have left? What crime would someone get seven years for? Why does no one believe her innocence?

STOP THE DRAMA AND CHECK THE UNDERSTANDING

Teacher-led questioning and discussion out of role to check that the group understand the area that the drama has moved into and the `facts' of the story.

MODEL

The teacher and a volunteer present an improvised scene between a journalist and a photographer who are planning the interview they intend to hold with Maria.

A model may help the group if they are unused to drama work or do not feel confident with the material.

PAIR WORK

In pairs A and B,
A = journalist.
B = photographer.
Together they plan the interview, in role, that will take place with Maria.

Here are some possible questions:
i   How might Maria feel after five years in prison?
ii   What might Maria do first?
iii Who might Maria want to see?
iv   Would things be the same?

The use of an interview as a way of developing drama following up suggestions from the group is important. It offers protection as no one has been asked to play Maria. The teacher's role also provides protection. Spontaneous improvisation, with the group as observers and participants in the situation.

WHOLE GROUP WITH TEACHER IN ROLE

TIR as editor calls for a report back from the newspaper staff. The use of TIR here and the questioning by the editor helps to build belief in the drama and also acts as a further check on the group's understanding of the task.

Drama Strategies

THE STORY OF MARIA

PAIR WORK

In the same pairs A and B,
A = journalist.
B = photographer.
Together they rehearse the interview, in role, with B taking the place of Maria.

This is a rehearsal for an event that is yet to happen. It must be clear to the students that they are journalists and photographers pretending to be Maria, a role- within-a-role. This is a distancing technique providing the students with an emotional protection.

At this point no one is being asked to play Maria, who has obviously undergone harrowing emotional and physical experiences. B is a photographer who works for a newspaper pretending to be Maria so that the journalist can rehearse his / her questions for when they meet Maria. This degree of protection is important.

PAIR WORK AND FROZEN PICTURE

In the same pairs A and B,
A = journalist.
B = photographer.
This time together they rehearse the photograph they will take with A taking the place of Maria. The photograph must suit the story they are writing.

Obviously for this B, the photographer, will be sculpting a frozen picture.

WHOLE GROUP WITH TEACHER DISCUSSION

❏ The teacher leads a discussion with the whole group out of role about what Maria might do on the day of her release. We are trying to build a picture of one very special day in Maria's life as if it were a feature in a newspaper. So each minute detail of what she does and where she goes is important.

❏ This should lead into a negotiation with the group about the 'facts' of the day in question. With consensus certain times and places can be agreed upon. This provides an opportunity for the students to invest in creating the drama.

The decision for what happens in the drama should be left to the group and negotiated towards a consensus. One of the scenarios that developed when we tried this work was that Maria was innocent and knew she had been framed but was not sure who by. She spent the whole day tracking down her friends carefully trying to piece together the events on the day of her arrest until she was sure she knew who had committed the crime. Then she went to face them.

WHOLE GROUP WITH TEACHER IN ROLE

TIR as Maria is interviewed by various pairs at different times of day. The rest of the group observe what emerges.

Again to protect the group it is better that the teacher play this role rather than one of the students. Although the teacher knows, because it has been planned together, where Maria is going and why, as Maria they may be reluctant to tell the truth to the reporters. It is up to the press to decide if and why she is lying.

THE STORY OF MARIA

WHOLE GROUP WITH TEACHER IN ROLE

❏ TIR as editor.
❏ SIR as photographers and journalists report back on their stories. They are also required to spend a short time to create a headline.

The work on the headline could be expanded to include liaison with the English department in order to look at journalistic style. That is, they could write an article with guidance and then examine, compare and contrast it with newspaper articles.

WHOLE GROUP WITH TEACHER IN ROLE

TIR as editor tells the group that although their stories are excellent they will not be printed. This is not the fault of the editor who blames an external power.

The teacher's use of 'second in power-chain' role is to disclaim all responsibility. The external agency could be the police, the owner of the paper, Maria's relatives etc. The importance of this is to challenge the group to defend their story and to build commitment to the drama.

NARRATION

The teacher narrates time passing. The journalists work on many other stories successfully but the idea for an article about Maria that they have never been allowed to write burns in their mind. For some time the position remains the same and the articles are not printed. However, suddenly things change.

Things change in accordance with the problem that has been developed earlier. If it was the police who stopped publication they now relax the laws, if it was Maria's family then 50 years pass and they have no further control, if it was the owner of the paper they have died and a new owner wants everything out in the open. The narrative device is to enable the group to move quickly on to their next important decision.

WHOLE GROUP WITH TEACHER IN ROLE

- ❏ TIR as editor is now prepared to allow the journalists to print, but on the clear understanding that they do so at their own risk.
- ❏ The group now have to make a moral decision. Should they sign the document accepting responsibility for their articles should the police (or anyone else) decide to prosecute. The teacher can prepare this document to fit the drama. This raises several questions. For example, 'Why is the story being suppressed?' 'What is being covered up?' 'Should they sign and risk personal prosecution?' 'Should the public be told?' 'What is the truth and what is suppression of the truth?' If they tell the truth they may also lay themselves open to threats and intimidation by the real culprits.

The editor must open the door but offer no sanction. The possibility to create the article is enabled but the journalists must take full responsibility for it.

Having a real document for them actually to sign adds tension and weight to this situation. As editor the teacher should work hard to make the group realize the full significance of their signing. If sued for example, they might lose their home, any savings, their family, and it could possibly cost them their career.

THE STORY OF MARIA

REFLECTION

Discussion and reflection on the
moral and social issues raised.

DEVELOPMENT

You may care to consider the following:

- ❏ On one day collect several different
  newspapers. How do they report
  the same event? What photographs
  do they use?
- ❏ Find out who owns each
  newspaper? Do you think there is
  any way these people could
  influence how the news is
  reported?
- ❏ What books or articles can you
  think of that have been suppressed
  by the British Government?
- ❏ Improvise a drama that focuses on
  how Maria's family was affected
  during the five years that she was
  imprisoned and the effect that the
  newspaper articles had on them.

THROUGH LINE LOGIC

Possible Developments

?

STIMULUS
Head of year talks
to students

PAIR WORK
Reps going to year council

PAIR WORK
Teachers going to
year council

WHOLE GROUP & TEACHER
Year council meeting

PAIR WORK
Head / Student

PAIR WORK
Student / Parent

FROZEN PICTURE
The stabbing

SMALL GROUPS
Parents and child

WHOLE GROUP & TEACHER
Reporters told to
interview witnesses

PAIR WORK
Interviews

**DRAMA RELATED
ACTIVITIES**
Invent the news report
of the disco

**INTEREST
COMING FROM THE
GROUP**

WHOLE GROUP & TEACHER
Assembly

DISCUSSION

STABBING AT A DISCO

General aims

To approach a difficult topic indirectly and to get students to see the social implications of violence. To show them that there is an overlap between the responsibilities of the school and the home.

What you need

A brightly coloured poster announcing a fictitious local club with `DISCO - FROM 8 TILL LATE' or something similar written on it (optional). See Resources 6 and 11 pages 132 and 137.

Strategies

Whole group with teacher in role, pair work, frozen picture, interviews.

ACTION POINTS

Stimulus

- ❑ TIR as a head of year.
- ❑ SIR as students at a school assembly.
- ❑ The head of year has a message from the head teacher who is annoyed that posters advertising a disco at a local club have appeared around the school. The head instructs all students to stay away from the club (it has a bad reputation for drugs and violence). The head of year completes year business, `reminding' students that forms should send two representatives to a year council meeting the next day. This will be their chance to have a say about the running of the school.

Although this lesson was devised in order to tackle a difficult subject it was deliberately organized to offer the potential for language work as well.

It's probably better not to have a poster at all if you cannot get a good one. Try other colleagues if you cannot create your own.

The situation of a school assembly allows TIR to convey a lot of information quickly. It also encourages good behaviour on the part of the class! This sometimes leads to interesting discussions on the purpose and nature of assemblies.

If your school does not have a year council or similar body then this can be an area for discussion. This project can also revitalize flagging existing councils.

PAIR WORK

In pairs A and B become two form representatives going to the meeting. Everybody is furious at the head teacher, who they say has no right to tell them what to do after school hours.

Improvise the conversation between these two on their way to the meeting. Make up a list of reasons why they should be allowed to go to the disco.

It may be useful to write the list of reasons down so that they can be referred to later. Although it is not essential for students to write out their ideas, the drama provides a vehicle which makes the writing important and often adds quality. They are not writing because they have been told to write but because it may help them to win their argument.

PAIR WORK

In pairs A and B become two teachers going to the meeting. Everybody is keen to support the head teacher, who they say has every right to tell the students what to do after school hours.

Improvise the conversation between these two on their way to the meeting. Make up a list of reasons why the students should not be allowed to go to the disco.

WHOLE GROUP WITH TEACHER IN ROLE

- ❏ The year council meeting.
- ❏ TIR as head of year has already made up the agenda for the meeting and wants to discuss something safe, for example uniforms. The students want to discuss the disco. The head of year is sympathetic but says there is nothing they can do about it. The head's decision is final.

It is probably more advisable to play the head of year than head, otherwise excessive hostility may reduce the progress of the drama. Equally the students may suggest the type of character they want you to play, which may range from sympathetic to authoritarian. This can also lead to useful discussion.

STABBING AT A DISCO

PAIR WORK

A = head teacher.
B = student.
B has to explain to A why they want to go to the disco. A listens but presents the reasons why this cannot be permitted.

Most students will share the annoyance at the head's interference out of school. However, it may be that the head's position can be understood.

PAIR WORK

In pairs A and B,
A = a student who has bragged to an older group of students that he / she will definitely be going to the disco and will be allowed to stay out late.
B = a parent who has heard terrible things about this disco.

A asks B if he / she can go.

FROZEN PICTURE

At the disco there is a stabbing.

In groups of about six students have to create two 'photographs' of the incident, one before and one after the event, as if there was someone there with a camera.

The technique of using frozen pictures stops any chance of physical violence.

SMALL GROUPS

One child was not allowed to go to the disco but went anyway. The parents find out when they see their child in a photograph in the local paper, taken immediately after the stabbing.

Act out the scene where the parents confront the child with this information.

It may be useful to involve other people as well, for example, police, neighbours, relatives, friends of the child.

> The idea of being caught out telling a lie is popular with most groups and they can usually sense the point of tension in the work. It is useful to point out to the group what they are doing when this happens. They are beginning to manipulate the form for themselves.

WHOLE GROUP WITH TEACHER IN ROLE

- ❏ TIR as editor of local newspaper.
- ❏ SIR as reporters.
  The reporters are told to interview anybody connected with the stabbing, for example, those present, passers-by, relatives, neighbours, police, local teachers.

> TIR as editor allows the teacher to give information about what journalism involves. Journalists can prepare the kinds of questions they will ask or even write them out.

PAIR WORK

In pairs A and B,
A = journalist.
B = interviewee.

The journalist interviews someone connected with the incident.

> This pair work is usually superficial at first. B often gleefully tells the journalist about the terrible things that have happened. However it is worth persevering and pointing out to the group how the people may really feel in this situation, especially if they knew the people involved, which is likely.

STABBING AT A DISCO

WHOLE GROUP WITH TEACHER IN ROLE

❏ TIR as head of year. This TIR should be used to set the tone for the work. The assembly should be presented in a low-key, serious and sad way.

❏ SIR at an assembly.
The head of year gives the details for the funeral. It is all very sad and highly regrettable. The family would appreciate a quiet affair. The younger sister of the victim is being sent to another school.

WHOLE GROUP WITH TEACHER DISCUSSION

Consider the students' original views of the head teacher's attitude to the disco. Have their views changed? Are school and home entirely separate?

This is an opportunity for the teacher to raise questions for the group to reconsider their original position.

DEVELOPMENT

You may care to consider the following:
❏ How accurate do you think the newspaper story will be?
❏ What events lead up to the stabbing at the disco?
❏ The court case of those involved.
❏ The fresh start in a new town for the victim's family.

ADVANCED ORGANIZER - *THE BOX*

Possible Developments

?

| STIMULUS TEACHER & VOLUNTEER Mime finding a box |

MODEL
Two volunteers add dialogue as scene is replayed

| QUESTIONING What happened ? |

INTEREST COMING FROM THE GROUP

| PAIR WORK Find out about the box |

| DISCUSSION What have we found out ? |

| PAIR WORK Spontaneous improvisation finding & opening the box |

| PAIR WORK Prepared improvisation Responding to contents |

| PRESENTATION & QUESTIONING |

| DISCUSSION Development ? |

| SMALL GROUPS Improvisation to develop work |

| REFLECTION |

THROUGH LINE LOGIC

THE BOX

General aims

To introduce ideas of theatrical form, character, decision making, problem solving through an awareness of questions.

What you need

Chalkboard and chalk or sugar paper and marker pens. See Resource 13 page 139.

Strategies

Mime, questioning, pair work, presentation.

ACTION POINTS

Stimulus

❏ The teacher with a volunteer who has already been primed to demonstrate at the front. The rest of the group are told to watch very carefully.

❏ Using mime the teacher and volunteer act out finding an imaginary box. They move the box around, each claiming it is theirs. Then suddenly one discovers how to open the box. At this stage nothing is taken out of the box. The mime finishes.

This lesson was devised to help the group develop their imagination and to demonstrate how that once they invest in the drama the work becomes much more absorbing.

QUESTIONING

❏ Teacher questioning to establish what has happened in the improvisation and how we know. Establish the difference between what has happened and how the effect was created. It may also be interesting to compare different observations as it is likely that some people will disagree on certain interpretations of the mime.

❏ Encourage the group to ask for more details about the characters. For example, who are they? Where are they? What are they doing? How do they find the box? Point out that these questions need answering, but they will be answered by them, not by you the teacher.

❏ Record their responses so that they can see what has been said and refer to this.

As ever when asking questions vary the type of question. Ask genuine questions which can receive a creative response. Value the answers you are offered.
For example,

Analysis
'What happened in the mime?'

Hypothesis
'From what you saw, to whom does the box belong?'

Evaluation
'What have you learned about the way you show size in mime from watching this?'

Synthesis
'They argued before but now that they have discovered something in the box what do you think will happen?'

Analogy
'Can you think of any other situations where two people both claim to own something?'

Deduction
'From what you have seen what type of box is this and how does it open? Demonstrate this to me.'

THE BOX

PAIR WORK

- ❏ In pairs students have two minutes to invent as much information as possible about this box.
- ❏ Stress that they must consider only the box they have seen mimed so far. It is important to negotiate towards a consensus of size and shape. A brief discussion of mime technique may also be appropriate. For example, keeping objects the same size, remembering where things are put and whether they are open or closed.

DISCUSSION

Teacher and group discussion. Using the chalkboard or sugar paper the teacher gathers information about the box.

Write up the ideas from the group to give them status. How big is the box? What is it made of? Is it light / heavy? etc.

PAIR WORK

Spontaneous improvisation, `What would you do if you found this box?' and `How would you open it?'

The quality of this work may be improved if you do not allow too much time and insist on serious work.

PAIR WORK

Prepared improvisation, which shows how you respond to what is in the box.

It may be important to discuss the range of feelings that could be demonstrated in response to the content of the box. This may be done:
i   through teacher demonstration
ii   through discussion
iii through the idea of detective work. For example, if you saw this reaction (a frozen picture of someone with a terrified expression on their face miming looking into a box) what type of thing might you expect to be in the box?

PRESENTATION

Sharing of prepared improvisations so that you can deepen belief and reinforce good ideas.

Teacher questioning to involve the audience in the examination of what is presented. Does the presentation give the effect that those presenting had wanted to achieve?

DISCUSSION

Negotiation with the group about how the drama might develop.

It is important to be genuine and go with the ideas of the group.

THE BOX

GROUP WORK

Group improvisations to develop the
work already produced.

REFLECTION

Examine with the group how a simple
basic structure has evolved in many
different directions. Stress how there
are as many different responses as
there are people in the room.

DEVELOPMENT

You may care to consider the
following:
❏ What happens if a third person
   comes along and claims the box
   is theirs?
❏ How might the same character
   approach the same box in different
   ways?
❏ What special power might the
   box have when you place objects
   inside it?
❏ Who has owned the box in the past
   and what curse have they placed
   upon it?

ADVANCED ORGANIZER - *INTERROGATION*

Possible Developments

?

THROUGH LINE LOGIC

TIR
Person interrogated

QUESTIONING

ACTION REPLAY

FROZEN PICTURE
Photograph

QUESTIONING

DISCUSSION

GROUP WORK
Before

GROUP WORK
After

GROUP WORK
Now

GROUP WORK
Shaping

PRESENTATION

REFLECTION

DRAMA RELATED ACTIVITIES
Writing character's confession

SOLO WORK
How people react when they are being watched

INTERROGATION

General aims

To encourage students to examine the requirements of the presentation section of GCSE drama. To consider the effect of decision making and its consequences.

What you need

Chalkboard and chalk or sugar paper and marker pens. See also Resource 8 page 144.

Strategies

Teacher in role, frozen picture, questioning, action replay, group work, discussion, presentation.

ACTION POINTS

Stimulus

TIR as person being interrogated. Sitting on a chair with arms wrapped around the body as if in a straightjacket. The following is said to a camera on the ceiling, 'I know you're looking at me, through that camera thing up there. You're too scared to come in here after last time. Look ... I promise to calm down and ... co-operate, but you must give me that photograph back.'

This structure was devised in response to a group of fifth form secondary students who were preparing for their drama GCSE. The work was carried out over a sequence of four weeks with two one hour and forty minute lessons each week. They were unclear about how to extend a simple idea into a longer piece of drama. They were also lacking confidence at asking questions beyond a basic superficial level. Throughout the work they were invited to make decisions and then made to stick to them. By parallel the decisions the characters made in the play were shown to effect others, yet the characters had to stick with the decision.

This TIR needs preparation. Obviously the words have to be learned, but it is worth exploring their delivery. Careful use of signing, pauses, slight physical movement will all add to the impact of this opening stimulus.

(continued on next page)

This particular style of TIR, where the character is in a different room, can only communicate through a microphone and camera, is restricted by a straightjacket, and watched through a one- way mirror also has another very important function! It allows the teacher to sit back and make an assessment of the students working in role. The teacher is in the role, but there will be occasions where the action is taking place outside the room.

OBSERVATION

The students watch this short scene.

They should be seated apart from the action, therefore not in a circle but possibly in a horseshoe with the action at one end.

QUESTIONING

Ask the students what they can tell you about this very brief scene. What do they know, what can they guess? What questions might it be appropriate to ask the character who is observed here?

The classification of the questions is important. Look at the section on questioning. By inviting the group to invent things they are beginning to shape the play for themselves, including defining their own role. This style of questioning also commits the group to the 'facts' of the scene as presented, and helps to build a consensus. Here are some examples of questions that might be asked at this stage: If we accept that what is said by the character is true then what is in the room?

(continued on next page)

INTERROGATION

What does this suggest is outside the room?
Where is this place?
Who might this character be?
Why is he / she here?
Who is outside?
What is in the photograph?
Why is it so important to the character?

ACTION REPLAY

Having established answers to some of the questions, certainly enough to have an idea of how the scene might develop, re-run the scene and attempt to move it on. Engage the students in role with the drama.

If the class have not yet committed themselves to a role you may need to point them towards a role by the way you respond in role. It will be crucial to establish also where they are and if it is likely that they will enter the room.

FROZEN PICTURE

The picture seems to be of great value to the character. What might it be a photograph of? Create a frozen picture of this image in two minutes.

It is important to see what they think would be important to the character from what they know so far.

This can be done as a whole group sculpture or in groups. If groups are chosen then remember these are what the photographs might be like, we do not yet know. It is up to the group to decide which photograph to use for the play.

QUESTIONING

View each of the `photographs' in turn and encourage the rest of the group to ask questions to find out the significance of the events.

It may be important to bring some of these scenes to life or hear the thoughts of the characters. Use a variety of questioning techniques to get the most out of each frozen picture. How do those contained within the picture react to each other? Who is responsible for taking the photograph?

DISCUSSION

What does this tell us about the character? What more have we learned about him / her and his / her family and friends?

Decide on one frozen picture which will now become the photograph referred to by the character at the beginning.

Attempt to build a more rounded personality than we have met previously. What predictions can be made about the way the character will behave now that more information is available?

GROUP WORK

In groups create a scene that shows how this character interacts with his / her family. Make it a time **before** the first scene takes place. The character may or may not appear.

If he / she does not appear then he / she must be referred to for the scene to show significantly how the characters relate to him / her. For example, the family group may be happily talking and enjoying a meal, until he / she returns and the atmosphere freezes over and there is silence.

INTERROGATION

GROUP WORK

In groups create a scene that shows how this character interacts with his or her family. Make it a time **after** the first scene takes place. The character may or may not appear.

It is important to remind the group of the 'facts' of the drama as it has unfolded. Their work must keep to the logic of what has gone before.

GROUP WORK

In groups create a scene that shows how this character came to be in the situation described by the first scene.

Ideas for this should have been developed by the previous work. The interests of the group should determine the outcome. Some possibilities might include espionage, insanity, drug or drink rehabilitation, 're-education', war.

GROUP WORK

In groups prepare all three of the above scenes and select a logical sequence to the events. Also include the frozen photograph. Rehearse these scenes so that they can be given as a presentation.

For their examination students will have to produce an extended piece so this is good practice. It is important to draw on skills they have learned in the past and in particular to remember about shaping a play - how and when to use flashbacks, economy of action, and various styles of presentation.

Throughout the group work the teacher should not direct the work but can be used as a resource. Encourage groups to stick by their decisions and see the consequences for other characters that the decision of one character may

(continued on next page)

make. For example, the decision the person interrogated makes may have grave implications for the person he / she informs against.

PRESENTATION

The groups present their work and the audience has the task of applying the examination criteria to their work to record positive examples of where the criteria have been met.

It is assumed that by the fifth year students are familiar with the assessment criteria, but if not they will obviously need a great deal of explanation. Assessment criteria vary between the exam boards, but for this work we concentrated on the following:

- ❏ To use dramatic stimuli for dramatic development.
- ❏ To use appropriate forms of verbal / non verbal communication.
- ❏ To adopt and sustain roles.
- ❏ To contribute, as an individual, to group development and realization of ideas.
- ❏ To demonstrate a practical understanding of the skills related to presentation.

Positive comments are requested to build on strengths and encourage the best work. Criticism will inevitably follow and can be very destructive if not handled well.

Point out what discoveries they have made and especially how they have manipulated the form. It is very important to establish the confidence of a group and instil in them the ability to see something through to completion.

INTERROGATION

REFLECTION

Teacher-led discussion about specific details of the play and about the fulfilment of the examination criteria. Return to the idea of making a decision and sticking with it - being able to stand up for your point of view, knowing what to say, and knowing when to back down.

DEVELOPMENT

You may care to consider the following:
- ❏ What happens if the character gets the photograph back and tears it into very small pieces?
- ❏ Who are the people doing the interrogation? Fill in their background.
- ❏ Create the dream or nightmare that the character has while awaiting interrogation.
- ❏ Read, or if possible watch, Pinter's *Mountain Language* and compare the effect of this play with the work created by the class.

THROUGH LINE LOGIC

Possible Developments

| ? |

GROUP WORK
Why do they need
a job ?

**INTEREST
COMING FROM THE
GROUP**

STIMULUS
Factory supervisor
welcomes applicants

DISCUSSION
Recap on work

PAIR WORK
Interviewer / Applicant

PAIR WORK
Friend / Applicant

DISCUSSION
The new job

NEGOTIATION
Plan of the factory

GROUP WORK
Creating the factory

WHOLE GROUP & TEACHER
The accident

FROZEN PICTURE
The machinist

WHOLE GROUP
Collection for victim

WHOLE GROUP & TEACHER
Factory supervisor
welcomes applicants

REFLECTION

THE FACTORY

General aims

To broaden pupils' understanding of `jobs', to consider power structures and working conditions.

What you need

A sheet of paper announcing the collection of money for an accident victim. See also Resource 9 page 135.

Strategies

Pair work, drama related activities - negotiated drawing, action replay.

ACTION POINTS

Stimulus

TIR as the factory supervisor welcoming applicants (SIR) for jobs at the factory.

It should become apparent from what the supervisor says that the factory has a bad reputation for accidents, but has recently been declared safe by inspectors of factories. Wages are low and conditions are poor. There is no union in the factory and the management are keen that this should remain the case.

This lesson was devised for a group of fourth year secondary students who were approaching their work experience placements and were unsure of both what they wanted to do and what would be expected of them. The lesson points out that workers should expect certain basic rights. It also invites investigation of some of the ways these rights have been achieved.

It is important that the TIR be the supervisor as they can report back from the management and yet not be held responsible for its decisions.

WHOLE GROUP WITH TEACHER DISCUSSION

The teacher recaps on the work
so far, what has been understood and
then encourages the group to make
some decisions about the drama. What
does the factory make? What sort of
vacancies might there be? How would
the supervisor decide on the suitability
of the applicants?

PAIR WORK

In pairs A and B,
A = interviewer employed by the
factory.
B = applicant who needs the job.

Using the information established in
the discussion conduct these
interviews.

When setting up these interviews
make them as 'formal' as possible
and attempt to evoke an appropriate atmosphere.

PAIR WORK

In the same pairs A and B,
A = a friend or relative who has heard
of the reputation of the factory
and is fearful for B's safety.
B = applicant who was successful at
getting the job.

B meets A and is overjoyed with his /
her good fortune and explains about
the new job. A shares his / her fears
with B.

THE FACTORY

WHOLE GROUP WITH TEACHER DISCUSSION

The teacher asks, 'What problems do the workers anticipate with their new job?' and 'What problems might this cause at home?' and 'Does it really matter if there is no union, especially as work is hard to come by?'

Depending upon the group it may be necessary to have information about unions, why they exist and why some work places do not encourage the formation of a union. There is a wealth of information available. Be imaginative, try to get this information across in an interesting way. If you have a willing history teacher introduce them in role as an 'expert' on unions so that the group can ask questions. Or invite a real trade unionist or union member to talk with the class about their experiences. Try to bring out both the advantages and disadvantages.

NEGOTIATION

The teacher negotiates the plan of the factory with the group. Together they draw this on the board or paper.

GROUP WORK

Using the plan that has been created the group sets up the factory. Each small group becomes part of the production line. The relationship to each individual machine and to the production line as a whole should be clear.

The group may need some time for this to be organized and run smoothly.

This is a type of dramatic playing. Depending on the experience of the group it may be preferable to organize 'machines' and only a few workers. The students playing the machines could then add the sounds and movements for the factory. Other groups may prefer a more naturalistic presentation.

WHOLE GROUP WITH TEACHER IN ROLE

- ❏ TIR as supervisor.
- ❏ SIR as factory workers.
- ❏ During a normal factory day the supervisor is overseeing the work when an accident occurs. An experienced worker, who has removed the safety guard to increase production and thus receive more pay, has caught his / her hand in the machine.

Run this improvisation through having primed one of the students to play the part of the machinist. You may be able to pick someone who has already chosen this type of work in their group.

FROZEN PICTURE

Before you repeat this improvisation examine the responses of the other factory workers. Organize this into a group frozen picture focusing on the machinist.

ACTION REPLAY

Re-run the improvisation, briefly pausing for the frozen picture. It may be possible to speak the thoughts of the onlookers.

Then resume the TIR, angry with them for stopping work. They will all be required to do unpaid overtime to make up for the work lost.

THE FACTORY

WHOLE GROUP IN ROLE WITHOUT TEACHER

After the supervisor leaves someone pins up a note announcing a collection of money for the accident victim. Someone else goes around the factory with a tin.

The management do not like to admit that accidents happen in this factory; they certainly do not like people stopping work to collect money for others who can no longer do their work.

The supervisor could return at any moment. Anyone found not working could face dismissal.

WHOLE GROUP WITH TEACHER IN ROLE

Repeat the opening improvisation. TIR as the factory supervisor welcoming applicants (SIR) for jobs at the factory.

With direct experience of the improvisation the applicants may be a little less enthusiastic. They may also wonder what has happened to the machinist who had the accident.

REFLECTION

❏ Was there a difference between the two improvisations?
❏ At any point did you notice tension in the drama. If so when, where, and why?
❏ What do you notice about how hierarchies work?

DEVELOPMENT

You may care to consider the following:

❏ The workers complain about safety standards in the factory. Their wages are cut. What should they do? The management claim that the factory is safe if the workers follow all the safety codes and do not remove the safety guards etc.

❏ Several workers visit the machinist in hospital. He / she has lost his / her hand due to the accident. The supervisor has not visited but has sent a message that the machinist will no longer be required at the factory. How can the workers help?

❏ A new machine arrives which is capable of replacing 16 workers. The factory owners want to install these machines. What is the response of the workers?

❏ The factory is making a loss. What should the owners do?

❏ One of the workers goes to the authorities about the factory. The factory claims that it is doing everything in its power to ensure a safe work place, but unfortunately one of the employees is sabotaging machinery. How can the case be proven?

Possible Developments

?

STIMULUS Shopkeeper does not want to prosecute

GROUP WORK
What happened in the past
to make the shopkeeper
not want to prosecute ?

WHOLE GROUP & TEACHER Case for the prosecution

**INTEREST
COMING FROM THE
GROUP**

PAIR WORK The dare

THREES Bullying

WHOLE GROUP & TEACHER Case conference

WHOLE GROUP & TEACHER The interview

GROUP WORK Improvisation

FURTHER DEVELOPMENT

THROUGH LINE LOGIC

THEFT IS COMPLICATED

General aims

To make students realize that the act of stealing has consequences for many people; it is not a simple act. To use the basic title / idea as a starting point for separate dramatic situations, all of which can lead to discussion.

What you need

Nothing.

Strategies

Whole group with teacher in role, pairs, threes, group work.

ACTION POINTS

Stimulus

- ❏ TIR as a shopkeeper who has caught a teenage girl shoplifting. The shopkeeper wants to prosecute.
- ❏ SIR as social workers who know the girl's family case history very well.
- ❏ The social workers try to persuade the shopkeeper not to prosecute.

This lesson was devised to help a group of students see that there is more than one point of view to any issue.

It is possible to use any of the action points as starts to different dramas.

This is a good fast start. Anything the students say about the character or background of the girl is true as long as it is consistent with what has previously been accepted and decided. It is a good idea to let the pupils win their argument. It makes an easy transition to the next roleplay.

Discussion can take place before, during and after the roleplay.

THEFT IS COMPLICATED

WHOLE GROUP WITH TEACHER IN ROLE

- ❏ TIR as a shopkeeper who has caught a teenage girl shoplifting. The shopkeeper does **not** want to prosecute.
- ❏ SIR as prosecution lawyers who are working for the police.
- ❏ The prosecution lawyers try to persuade the shopkeeper to prosecute.

PAIR WORK

In pairs A and B,
A = teenager.
B = teenager.
B dares A to steal something from a shop.

This work can be preceded by reasons why people steal.

THREES

In threes A,B and C,
A = older student.
B = older student.
C = victim of bullying.
C is bullied into stealing and is blackmailed for this by A and B.

This work needs to be preceded with a story based on the notion of one bad deed leading to another, also linking this to blackmailing and its consequences. A suggested story which is also a true one is:
A and B are older pupils who threaten to beat up C unless she steals something from a shop. After C has stolen the thing A and B tell C that the shop has a video camera and that the theft was certainly recorded on film. However, they say that the shopkeeper would probably only check the film and identify C if somebody warned her / him. A and B blackmail C. Should C submit to the blackmail?
What happens if she doesn't?
What happens if she does?
Why have A and B done this?

WHOLE GROUP WITH TEACHER IN ROLE

- ❏ TIR as chief social worker.
- ❏ SIR as social workers.
- ❏ This is a case conference to consider the control a family (invented) has over their child who has recently truanted, stolen and associated with `undesirables'. Should the teenager be put into care?

A family `case study' can be prepared before the lesson in as much detail as is felt necessary. Written documents can contribute positively to the belief in the drama. It is important that the group understands that this is an invented family, specifically created for this drama.

WHOLE GROUP WITH TEACHER IN ROLE

- ❏ TIR as job applicant.
- ❏ SIR as panel of interviewers.
- ❏ Interviewers know that the job applicant has previous convictions for theft.

This is a deliberately chosen low status role for the teacher which invites students to tackle the issue of `rehabilitation' from a position of power. The teacher should chose an occupation that both they and their class will feel confident with. Students tend to want to give an offender a second chance and are therefore challenged by the role given them.

THEFT IS COMPLICATED

GROUP WORK

In groups A, B, C, D, E, F, G.
A is bullied for money by B and C who are older pupils.

D is best friend of A.

E is new pupil expelled from the last school for stealing.

F is a teacher who has had money stolen during a lesson attended by A, D and E.

G is the head of year who automatically suspects E.

Improvise the scene and develop it.

This action point has a detailed list of roles which should not be seen as the only way of tackling this situation that is. how dishonesty has unseen consequences. To introduce this particular situation the teacher could tell the story rather than allocate the roles, for example, a student is expelled from one school for stealing, she goes to her new school where she is falsely accused of stealing. How could this happen? Thus leaving the majority of the story to the students.

DEVELOPMENT

You may care to consider the following:
- ❏ Invent a piece of surveillance `film' that shows someone stealing from a shop.
- ❏ Think of a situation when you believe it is right to steal. Improvise this scene and its consequences.
- ❏ Invent the trial for someone accused of stealing.
- ❏ Improvise a scene where a peasant has `stolen' water from the royal fountain, the only place left in the drought-stricken land where drinking water can be obtained. [See the story *'The Kings Fountain'* by Lloyd Alexander, first published 1971 in the United States by E.P. Dutton, New York.]

ADVANCED ORGANIZER - WAXWORKS

Possible Developments

| ? |

STIMULUS
Discussion: visits to
a waxworks

STORYTELLING
The visitor to the waxworks

GAME
Statues

STATUS GAME

WHOLE GROUP & TEACHER
Caretaker

**INTEREST
COMING FROM THE
GROUP**

MODEL
Sculpting a waxwork

PAIR WORK
Creating the wax models

GROUP WORK
Tableaux of a horror scene

PRESENTATION

WHOLE GROUP & TEACHER
Manager shows
visitors around

STORYTELLING

GROUP WORK
Dramatizing the story

REFLECTION

THROUGH LINE LOGIC

WAXWORKS

General aims

To help establish personal physical control, listening skills, group skills and awareness; to develop a sense of atmosphere and imagination; storytelling.

What you need

Story about waxworks (see below), candle (optional). See also Resource 18 page 143.

Strategies

Storytelling, game, model, whole group with teacher in role.

ACTION POINTS

Stimulus

Generate a discussion which allows students to relate their own visits to Madame Tussauds or any similar exhibition.

Prompt with questions like, What are waxworks? Who's been to see waxworks? What sort of people will you find displayed as waxworks?

This lesson was devised to encourage a group of students who though confident in expressing themselves verbally, were inhibited about using movement and facial expression.

STORYTELLING

Tell the story of *The Visitor to the Waxworks*. This is a story about someone who responds to a challenge to spend a night alone in a chamber of horrors. When he / she does so the figures come to life. Next day the person challenged, who had been strong and unafraid, is found cowering in a corner. He / she is so terrified he / she cannot even speak.

An ability to dim lights or blackout the room is useful. A lighted candle creates a superb atmosphere for telling the story.

GAME

Teach the class the game of statues. Play the version at first where they become individual statues. The group move around in various manners. At a given signal (verbal, whistle, handclap) all FREEZE! They must hold the frozen position as if they were an exhibit in a waxworks.

Later you may care to try the same exercise, but with group statues.

WHOLE GROUP WITH TEACHER IN ROLE

This extends the game into drama. This time the game of wax models is played so that they come alive but must freeze when directly looked at. TIR as the caretaker with a torch, who tries to catch models out when moving. If they are caught out they melt when the torch light hits them.

This will be recognized as a modified version of 'Grandmother's Footsteps' or 'Peep behind the Curtain'. The first time round the figures will leap forward; stress the need for minute and slow movements as these are more effective and creepy.

MODEL

The teacher demonstrates with a volunteer how to 'sculpt' the volunteer into various shapes.

It is important to experiment with level and shape. Remember to include sculpting of facial expression, but only if the group can deal with this sensitively.

WAXWORKS

PAIR WORK

In pairs A and B,
A = a wax model.
B = someone who manipulates A into a variety of positions or poses.

Decide on a pose for A. Freeze, then reverse roles.

Allow time for the pairs to experiment. At first you may get some ridiculous positions and possibly a deliberate attempt to sculpt the partner into an awkward shape. Persevere and stress the need for co-operation and shapes that will be useful to the drama.

GROUP WORK

Continue with the theme of statues on display and encourage groups to create a group tableaux of a horror scene. Display. Visitors gather round to examine tableaux.

PRESENTATION

Show one group sculpture at a time and have the rest of the group arrive as visitors to the exhibition. Remind them of the gallery rules; they are allowed to walk around the exhibition but not to touch.

WHOLE GROUP WITH TEACHER IN ROLE

TIR as manager or creator of the waxworks who shows a group of visitors around a number of tableaux.

What happens?

Allow for responses and suggestions from the group. The TIR may have to hint at a dark secret hidden in the creation of the waxwork figures.

STORYTELLING

Telling the story around the circle. Continuing the theme of waxworks, a candle is passed around the circle as each person contributes to the story.

Try a variety of stories which respond to the drama. You may focus on the work done so far or on those parts of the story that are yet to be uncovered. For example, you could take one of the waxworks and relate their history. What happened when they first came to life? What things have they seen? What secrets have they overheard from the visitors? What adventures have they been on?

WAXWORKS

GROUP WORK

Let the groups decide which of the stories attracts them and give them the task of turning these stories into drama.

Try to steer them away from repetition of the original drama. Encourage the group to use their own creativity and maintain the atmosphere that has been generated.

REFLECTION

Analyze the work that has been completed and pay careful attention to the skills that have been used. Try to be precise about successful moments in the work. When was the atmosphere successful, when was it broken? Why? Which statues captured the imagination? Why? How were they shaped?

Encourage the group to consider what skills they have used in this work that they might not usually pay attention to and suggest they use these techniques more often.

It is often said at GCSE level that while verbal dexterity is amply demonstrated many students do not pay enough attention to movement and expression.

DEVELOPMENT

You may care to consider the following:
- ❏ Where else do statues appear? How could this inform another piece of drama?
- ❏ Why do people make statues or waxworks of other people? List the qualities that you would use to select someone for sculpting.

- ❏ What happens in the waxworks after it has been closed to the public?
- ❏ Suppose one of the waxworks characters was scared of all the others, what might happen?

Possible Developments

?

STIMULUS 1999

QUESTIONING

PAIR WORK Old / young in 1999

QUESTIONING

FROZEN PICTURE The day in 1999 when everything went wrong for everyone

QUESTIONING & SHADOWING

WHOLE GROUP & TEACHER 'Free passage to a new world'

FROZEN PICTURE Who Goes ? Who Stays ?

FROZEN PICTURE 'How life might be different'

INTEREST COMING FROM THE GROUP

THROUGH LINE LOGIC

1999 – A LOOK TO THE FUTURE

General aims

This structure is designed to introduce the topic of emigration. It depends upon the distancing effect of time to offer protection for the students.

What you need

Chalkboard and chalk or poster sized paper and coloured marker pens. See also Resource 19 page 143.

Strategies

Questioning and shadowing, frozen picture.

ACTION POINTS

Stimulus

Chalkboard showing 1999.

This lesson was specifically designed to stimulate interest and imagination.

If you do not have a chalkboard use any similar method to record information with your groups.

You can select any future date you feel is significant - 2001, 2010, 2999. When we chose 1999 it was because the students with whom we were working would be 21 in that year.

1999 – A LOOK TO THE FUTURE

TEACHER-LED QUESTIONING

`How might life be different in 1999?'
Discussion in pairs – ideas gathered on
board. Teacher negotiates towards a
consensus.

The teacher should remain neutral,
receiving ideas from the group and
valuing each contribution.

As ever when asking questions vary
the type of question asked. Ask
genuine questions which can
receive a creative response. Value
the answers you are offered. For
example,

Analysis
`How would you describe the world
now? Good, bad, happy, sad,
clean, polluted?'

Hypothesis
`How might life be different in
1999?'

Evaluation
`What have you learned about the
way things are now that can help
you guess how life will be in
1999?'

Synthesis
`In the future if a young person and
an old person talked together do
you think they would share the
same point of view?'

Analogy
`Can you think of any other
situations where people have
travelled into the future?'

Deduction
`From what you have seen of
science fiction type films which do
you think offers the most likely
version of the future?'

PAIR WORK

In pairs A and B,
A = old person in 1999.
B = young person in 1999.
A tells B how it used to be.
B says why it is better now.

QUESTIONING

The teacher gathers information and tests the drama through shadow role.

The use of shadow role is to avoid the standard report back. The role will be indicated by the pair work. For example, the teacher may momentarily become a journalist or historian.

FROZEN PICTURE

In groups create a frozen picture for which the caption might be: 'The day in 1999 when everything went wrong for everyone.'

Frozen pictures tend to work best under strict time constraints. Try to allow no more than two minutes.

QUESTIONING AND SHADOWING

Questions asked of the frozen pictures in order to establish exactly what has been created. Remember to take advantage of these different forms of questioning and shadowing:
- ❏ by the teacher.
- ❏ by the rest of the group.
- ❏ by another person answering for each character.
- ❏ by going back further in time, or forward that is.

Make a new picture.
- ❏ by each person speaking a line
- ❏ by bringing the picture to life.

This is to build belief and deepen the drama. The teacher should select activities felt to be most appropriate to the age and experience of the group.

WHOLE GROUP WITH TEACHER IN ROLE

TIR holding letters.
'Citizens, I am here to tell you about an opportunity beyond your wildest dreams. I am authorized to offer you free passage to a new world beyond our solar system where there is wealth for the taking. The offer is only available today so you must make up your minds quickly. Step forward and sign up for the journey of a lifetime.'

TIR is used as a device to move towards the learning area. For example, the teacher may become a representative from a government agency explaining about the opportunities in another country - thus directing the learning towards emigration.

The letters hold a symbolic value. They are 'official' and commit the signatory to a one-way passage. Their power should be felt in the drama.

FROZEN PICTURE

Create a frozen picture of those who choose to stay; and those who choose to leave. In the picture pay particular attention to objects held by various people. Those leaving face a luggage restriction, what personal possessions do they take? Those staying may have received gifts from friends or relatives leaving.

Again the symbolic value of these objects is important. The group should be encouraged to invest meaning into these items.

DEVELOPMENT

The teacher and group can decide how the drama should develop from here. The following areas may prove worth further investigation:

❑ Arriving on the new planet and feeling that you do not belong.
❑ Not being able to find work or suitable accommodation - despite being told both were plentiful.
❑ Missing 'home'.
❑ Receiving abuse from those already resident on the new planet.

Possible Developments

?

| STIMULUS
Anecdote |
| --- |

| QUESTIONING |

| PAIR WORK
Lifestory |

| SPOTLIGHTING |

| WHOLE GROUP & TEACHER
Time Travel Inc.
welcomes |

| STOP THE DRAMA
Check understanding |

| ACTION REPLAY |

| MODEL
Time to do again |

| STOP THE DRAMA
Check understanding |

| ACTION REPLAY |

| QUESTIONING |

| GROUP WORK
Creating the scenes |

| PRESENTATION |

DRAMA RELATED ACTIVITY
Personal writing in role
of a character who wants
a second chance to do
things differently

**INTEREST
COMING FROM THE
GROUP**

THROUGH LINE LOGIC

TIME TRAVEL INC. – A SENSE OF THE PAST

General aims

This structure is designed to introduce the concept of time. It is specifically designed to find out what the group already know about time and to challenge assumptions.

What you need

Nothing. However there are two useful reference points:
1 Ray Bradbury's story *A Sound of Thunder* in *The Golden Apples of the Sun*, Panther Books, 1977.
2 Steven Spielberg's film *Back to the Future*, Universal Studios, 1986. See also Resource 10 page 136.

Strategies

Whole group with teacher in role, spotlighting, action replay, using a model, presentation.

ACTION POINTS

Stimulus

❑ Anecdote. Teacher asks the question, 'Has there ever been anything in your life that you wish you could do over again?' Then immediately answers it himself / herself with an anecdote (real or imaginary).

❑ Remember this is a drama lesson. Students need protecting. Do not allow other members of the group to ridicule those making suggestions. Accept individual contributions if offered, though it may be better to plant the suggestion and then work in role. It is the idea that is significant.

This work was devised for a fourth year secondary GCSE examination group. The teacher wanted to stretch the group and give them something 'hard' to grapple with. Consequently, he chose the concept of time. Rather than maintain an abstract approach the teacher set the work in what he hoped would be familiar territory for the group who were confident and enjoyed drama lessons.

TIME TRAVEL INC. – A SENSE OF THE PAST

TEACHER-LED QUESTIONING

'What things do we regret?'
This is discussed in pairs and then ideas are gathered on the board by the teacher. Imaginative suggestions should be encouraged. Then the teacher should negotiate towards a consensus.

The teacher should remain neutral, receiving ideas from the group and valuing each contribution. Remember, protection is the most important thing here. Do not force anyone to answer. Students may be understandably reluctant to commit themselves. Allow and encourage answers in the third person such as, 'Well I had a friend who ...' or, 'Someone once told me ...' Make this a general discussion rather than a personal one.

PAIR WORK

In pairs invent a character who, if given the chance, would do something in their life differently. Create a scene where this person tells their story. This piece of work will include actor / storyteller, flashback, and improvisation.

Insist on a creative / imaginative response, so that the students are protected by a role.

SPOTLIGHTING

Teacher interrupts the whole group to catch glimpses of the work in progress by focusing on various pairs. Having established the idea it is now appropriate to move on.

This is not a complete presentation, merely an attempt to check on the work in progress.

TIME TRAVEL INC. – A SENSE OF THE PAST

WHOLE GROUP AND TEACHER IN ROLE

`You have been carefully selected by our computer for this once in a lifetime opportunity. Time Travel Inc. are offering you the chance to travel to any moment of your past and remain there for 24 hours. Whilst there you will be able to review actions that you have taken in the past. You may not, of course, interfere, only observe. Any questions?'

It is vital that the teacher signs that this is not a normal trip and that people **do** interfere in the past. The students should be suspicious of such an offer. However, you do want them to take it up.

STOP THE DRAMA AND CHECK THE UNDERSTANDING

Out of role establish what has happened.
❑ What role was I playing?
❑ What sort of person was he / she?
❑ Did you trust him / her?
❑ Who were you meant to be?
❑ When was the play set?
❑ How do you think things might develop?

This is to check the level of understanding and invite everyone to share the same play. The teacher also has the opportunity to gauge the level and direction of interest.

ACTION REPLAY

Re-run the drama and extend the work with the new knowledge gained through discussion.

The group can be pushed further this time as they will be more confident and more knowledgeable about the play.

Drama Strategies

TIME TRAVEL INC. – A SENSE OF THE PAST

MODEL

Teacher and volunteers.

Portray a frozen moment in time. It is the time of the incident. The teacher, in role as the time traveller, narrates the events of the scene as it comes to life. It is the scene of a mugging. The time traveller, much younger then, is played by one of the volunteers. He is scared, unsure what to do. He passes by on the other side of the road, not daring to intervene.

The strong moral tone of this should be obvious to the group.

The incident does not have to be a mugging, especially if the group can suggest their own situation.

STOP THE DRAMA AND CHECK THE UNDERSTANDING

Out of role establish what has happened.
- ❏ What was the traveller's responsibility?
- ❏ Why didn't he / she stop?
- ❏ What would they have done?

ACTION REPLAY

Re-run the drama and this time the traveller intervenes.

QUESTIONING

Time Travel Inc. issued a warning not to interfere in the past.

❑ Why?
❑ Might this have any affect?
❑ How?

GROUP WORK

To create and present three scenes:

i   Frozen picture, narration, brought to life scene of original situation.

ii Frozen picture, narration, brought to life scene with intervention of the time traveller.

iii A scene that explains how life is different on return to the present time.

This should be their own work and they should be encouraged to consider the elements necessary for good presentation.

PRESENTATION

The groups present their scenes to each other, but the audience is given a frame. They are a tribunal watching criminals defend themselves. They have broken a very strict code which says it is forbidden to interfere with the past. The watchers must decide if the interference was justified (that is, motivated by a desire to help others) or not justified (motivated out of selfishness). The punishment is death.

The deliberate choice of a frame for the audience in which decisions are to be made opens several possibilities. The audience can be invited to comment not just on the way the work was presented, but also its content. It stops the audience being passive as they have an active role. The teacher should continue the whole class play in between these testimonials. Finally it returns us to the moral question.

Drama Strategies　　　　　　　　　　*LESSON STRUCTURES*

TIME TRAVEL INC. – A SENSE OF THE PAST

DEVELOPMENT

You may care to consider the following:
- ❑ Why do Time Travel Inc. offer this service?
- ❑ How might it be used illegally?
- ❑ What might happen if you stayed longer than 24 hours?
- ❑ Suppose you could never return to your present. How would you fit into your own past?
- ❑ Why does interference with the past carry such a harsh punishment?
- ❑ How might the use of symbolic objects or ritual be introduced into the work?
- ❑ How does the information provided by the ghosts in Charles Dickens' *A Christmas Carol* affect the behaviour of Scrooge? Why is this?

THROUGH LINE LOGIC

Possible Developments

?

STIMULUS Discussion of what to make a video about

DRAMA RELATED ACTIVITY
Watch a sample of
videos & examine the
way they
are put together

GROUP WORK Improvisation of content

INTEREST
COMING FROM THE
GROUP

GROUP WORK Scripting

GROUP WORK Rehearsal

PRESENTATION

ROUGH SHOOT

SCREENING APPRAISAL

FINAL SHOOT

MAKING A VIDEO DRAMA

General aims

To help students make realistic decisions related to their drama by giving a firm external discipline and providing an end product for general appraisal and criticism.

What you need

Video camera / recorder, VTR and monitor. See also Resource 14 page 140.

Strategies

Video, group work, presentation.

ACTION POINTS

Stimulus

The group are invited to make a video drama that has relevance to their lives or that they feel is important to make.

Sometimes more choice is less. Make the choice of content theirs if they have an idea that they are excited by. Otherwise you may need to prime them.

For example: schools of the future can be a good starter as you can use the school for all location shots, taking the idea of exaggerating the way things are now and projecting them into a mid-term future. All order has broken down and a group of fifth formers control the school with drugs; the school has been converted into a waxworks museum of the way things used to be.

This lesson was devised in response from many students who wanted to learn how to use the video equipment properly. Students are often disappointed with their results because they have not spent enough time planning or researching what they want to make.

Ensure that you are familiar with your equipment. Try it out beforehand. Look confident!

GROUP WORK

Prepare and present a drama that might be suitable for video.

The teacher should explain the limitations of the medium. Also restrict the time, both of the rehearsal and the finished piece. If this is a first attempt restrict their work to between 5-15 minutes of `finished' video.

GROUP WORK

- ❏ From their practical work they will need to prepare shooting scripts.
- ❏ It's a good idea to prepare `blank' shooting scripts for use.
- ❏ They will need considerable help to make an economic script. It is important to be sure of your locations and the times that they are available. The following will enhance the work if they are available: props, background music, sound effects, costume.
- ❏ Do an example of a script with them, then let them prepare their own.

MAKING A VIDEO DRAMA

GROUP WORK

Bringing the drama to life from the shooting scripts. Preparing for recording.

When setting up the camera / recorder at this point make it clear that you will be doing all the filming at present but they will each have a go at looking through the view-finder. You don't need to film anything at this stage. In this session the pupils will start getting used to the equipment. When they are familiar with the equipment they may want to record the work for themselves.

PRESENTATION

Each group in turn presents their work as it will be recorded. The teacher leads a discussion evaluating the work encouraging the class to compare the two different media (mime and video).

Discuss what people noticed looking through the view-finder. For example, people looking at the camera, background noise, drama out of the camera frame, `corpsing', messing about. The video imposes its own discipline.

One obvious point, mime is an accepted convention in drama, but on video it looks wrong. When recording, if a character needs to go through a doorway a real one must be used.

ROUGH SHOOT

Filming the 'roughs' of each group's presentation.

Experience dictates that it is easier to organize this if everyone watches each scene being shot. The whole group must be involved during 'rough' takes. To be silent is as important as anything else, but the audience could be in role - however minimal. Perhaps film critics, potential sponsors or backers.

Try and get other teachers to take the parts of adults. They can also take the part of minders if you have to take a small group to film a scene outside the drama room. Keep your locations as close to the drama room as possible or arrange special sessions.

SCREENING

Appraisal of the 'roughs'. Has the conception been realized?
Are any changes necessary before the final shoot?

This session should be in a classroom set up for showing the video. Get the pupils to be as honest as possible in their assessment of the scene(s) and advise them to change things that are glaringly ridiculous, impractical, etc. Any embarrassment needs careful handling by the teacher. The students must feel emotionally protected.

MAKING A VIDEO DRAMA

Depending upon the group the discussion of the work may need special handling. Usually time spent in this session will reduce time wastage later.

FINAL SHOOT

❏ Final rehearsal and filming.
❏ Film the titles before you start filming the drama and credits last of all. Rehearse each scene as though it were being filmed. Get your minders in again. You don't have to shoot in sequence although this will make your editing easier. You can edit from your machine to a normal VHS set-up or using two VTRs.

Teachers often miss the opportunity to repeat work. If shown that a good result is possible most groups will wish to redo their `roughs'. It is nearly always worth the trouble.

If you are not sure how to manage the editing ask the school technician if you have one or get in touch with the local Teachers' Centre. Dubbing a sound-track, making titles and credits etc can all usually be done in school and usefully involve other departments.

DEVELOPMENT

You may care to consider the following:
❏ Why not offer this service to other departments? Or to record a school event?
❏ Record a day in the life of your school.
❏ Make a commercial, for a real or imaginary product. Or a warning against something.
❏ Create your own video box where people can speak their mind.

TECHNIQUES / STRATEGIES
TEACHER IN ROLE

So long as you feel comfortable using the teacher in role strategy there will be many advantages. You will be inside the play with the students and can therefore actively affect what is happening from the **inside**. You can, of course, stop the action at any time and resume the role of teacher to address the students. However, there are so many advantages to working in role that the necessity for doing this will diminish. Examples of the teacher working in role with the whole group can be found in, `Drugs', `Hillside Unit', `The story of Maria', `Stabbing at a disco', `Interrogation', `The factory', `Theft is complicated', `Waxworks', `1999', `Time Travel Inc.'.

The type of role that you chose to take on can vary in many ways. For example, you can select roles which reflect different levels of status:

❏ High - as with a role similar to that of teacher, where you are in charge of something: a custom's officer, newspaper editor, factory supervisor, warden.
❏ Second in command - so that you can disclaim responsibility and pass the buck: the editor (with a publisher), senior warder.
❏ Medium - a role equivalent to the rest of the group: a member of the gang, an inmate, factory worker.
❏ Low - a role lower than that played by the group, often requiring help: the shopkeeper who does not want to prosecute, the cleaner in the factory, the parent whose child will not listen to them and does as he / she pleases, a member of the Drug Squad who has become dependent on drugs.

You can select roles which help to model a style of performance to the group. For example, if you play the warden in `Hillside Unit', you could attempt to intimidate the `inmates' with your language and physical presence. Such an overpowering character will expect only one type of response from `inmates' and an accompanying formalised language register. Similarly, when playing the person that is interrogated in `Interrogation' the language used will give the clue that this is modern day. But if an older style of language is used and the talk is of taxes required by the King, instead of photographs, the group may be persuaded that the play has moved into the past.

Another advantage with teacher in role is the economy it gives to the drama work. If you are experienced with the strategy and comfortable with the group you will be able to start the play directly in role and allow the group to find out about the play from what your character does and says. Sometimes this will be preferable to telling the group everything in advance. A clear example of this is the `Interrogation' structure.

TEACHER IN ROLE

Once you are working inside the play with the rest of the group it becomes easier to focus their attention and move them all into the same play. This will then make it easier for the teacher to read the group and discover what their real interests are and where the play should move next. An example of teacher in role beginning to focus the group can be seen in `Hillside Unit'. The more the warden shouts and storms about the failure of the two inmates to report to his / her office the more likely it is that the group will band together against this outrageous person.

In the `Hillside Unit' a second person in role was also used. This is another useful device. This could be another teacher, someone who has specially come into the school for this lesson, a student from another group, or a student from this lesson. The second role is often used to give a commentary on the first, and therefore is much closer to the role played by the students. In this case the senior warder `appears' to be friendly and trying to help them.

Another element that is often forgotten is the protection offered by a role within a role. This device occurs throughout Shakespeare and many other playwrights' work and is an important drama strategy. An example of this occurs in `Hillside Unit' when the investigative team pretend to be something else. Or it might be that in `The story of Maria' the journalists pretend to be something other than journalists in order to get their story.

SIGNING

Signing is the way that you use facial expression, body language and the spoken word. Effectively used it is one of the best ways of moving the group towards the art form. One way to establish this technique with your group is to demonstrate to them how you can say exactly the same words but mean two opposite things. For example, look directly at one of the group, look at their eyes, smile, hold out your hand and shake theirs, then say, 'Helen, I'm really pleased to see you!' in a bright friendly tone. Then look at someone else, look away, look down at the floor, frown, hold out your hand reluctantly and shake their's without enthusiasm, then say, 'Peter, I'm really pleased to see you!' with a crack in your voice and a hollow tone. Then ask the group which of the two they thought you were pleased to see. If you have signed well they should notice a distinct difference and be able to practice this for themselves.

Within the drama signing can be used to give clues. Children are constantly reading adult faces in schools to find out how they should proceed next, so it is no surprise to find that they are very quick to pick up the slightest clue in the drama. For example, as the police spokesperson in 'Drugs' the teacher will be saying that the police are in control of the situation but signing, perhaps by fidgeting and looking as if they do not believe their own words, that this is not the case. This gives the students in role as journalists something to pick up on in the drama.

Signing is often a good way of encouraging the group to become suspicious. If you are a character whose role is to sit on a chair in a room and keep still, it will soon become obvious that something is on your mind if you say nothing but constantly check your watch and look anxiously at the door. In fact, as teacher you could start the play like this and then ask the group to suggest one character each to come through the door, which they, of course, get to play.

In this way signing introduces tension, and it may be that the role signs too much and pushes the drama too far in one direction. In 'Time Travel Inc.' the travel agent from Time Travel Inc. must sign that this is a once in a lifetime opportunity, but not without its dangers. If the dangers are emphasized too much the travellers may decide not to take the trip.

DISCUSSION

Discussions may take place in or out of role. Often by placing students in role you can encourage a more lively debate. Partly this is due to the protection that is offered, as the group are enabled to say things that are appropriate for their character and therefore not necessarily what they believe. If you deliberately select roles that are almost opposite in the way they think the debate may get very lively. It may, however, remain in a rather stereotypical area.

Within the drama it may be necessary to build in a structure so that people talk one at a time. In this way each contribution can be equally valued rather than the loudest voice always dominating. A court-room gives an obvious structure, but you could establish a rule to suit your situation. For example, on a desert island it could be the person who holds the conch who has the 'right' to speak. The conch is passed around the circle so that everyone has an equal chance to say something. If you want to speak you do so holding the conch. If you do not you pass the conch on.

A group may report back to the class about an aspect of the work in role. A discussion may be had in role between two opposing characters. Characters could be hot-seated or asked to reproduce scenes in slightly different ways. Groups could be encouraged to select the moment that they felt was most important in their play and produce this as a frozen picture.

Do not feel that discussions about drama work always need to come at the end of the lesson. There are often opportunities during the work, both in and out of role, to discuss what is happening. If you don't check on what the students think is happening you may be creating a completely different version of the play to the one they hold in their heads. Consequently you will be in a very poor position to direct the learning area.

An obvious point, but one often forgotten: discussions work best when participants have something to say. An isolated question thrown out to a group with no context may not elicit a response. A question directly responding to a common experience will be much more successful. Ask them to comment upon what they think they have learned. What did they feel was their major contribution in this work? What did they find most successful about someone else's work?

Another factor is the reluctance of some group members to speak in a public arena. Here it is important to build up the discussion in discrete stages. Ask a question for the group to consider in pairs. Then ask another question or series of questions for the group to consider, this time joining two pairs together. Suggest each four elect one person to represent the responses from the group to the whole group. Then hold the whole group discussion, ensuring that each group has a chance to report back. In this way those intimidated by the whole class discussion will have had an opportunity to test out what they think in advance. They may then feel strong enough to say what they want to, or, if not, they will have someone to speak for them. This way of organizing a discussion also means that more people are talking for more of the time.

GROUP WORK

There are many occasions within a drama lesson where it may be necessary for the whole group to split up into smaller ones. When this is the case you may find it useful to have a prearranged signal that lets the group know that they should then be silent and await further instructions. If you take the trouble to establish this as a way of working with your groups it will amply repay the effort. It will mean that you are always in control. The group will then have a better experience in drama lessons and want to make the system work. Obviously, whatever signal you choose must be negotiated with the group. Once they agree to it make them keep to their agreement.

The best signals are ones where the group take responsibility in an active way. For example, we have found that once the group agree that the best signal would be for the teacher to stand in the middle of the room with his / her hand up, they actively take on the responsibility of stopping work and wait to listen to what the teacher has to say. This is preferable to the teacher shouting above the noise or wildly blowing on a whistle - but only if it works. The teacher must shoulder the responsibility of finding something that works with their class.

Once you have this control you can stop the groups at any point and introduce new information into their work or give new instructions. This tends to interrupt the flow of work far less than calling everyone back to a certain point. However, recalling everyone at points during the lesson may also serve a useful function.

Groups can be of any size that is practicable for the space and teacher concerned. If there are instructions to be given about the role to be undertaken it is probably a good idea to label each person. For example, with pairs call them A and B; with threes call them A, B and C; with fours call them A, B, C and D, etc. This both aids the delivery of instructions and helps commit a student to a role.

The important point about group work is that everyone is working at the same time. Nobody is exposed to the full glare of the class. This often means that groups are more confident about experimenting with their work and trying out things that they are not yet sure they can achieve. This is a very important part of their development in drama.

While the groups are focused on the drama work and contributing to its development it is interesting to note the skills that individuals are using. Who is leading the group? Who supporting? Who is taking responsibility for those who do not understand, say little, or are shy? Who organizes the work space? Who defends their point of view against the rest of the group? Who is quick to find compromises in the interest of moving the work forward? Who deliberately blocks the work and takes a delight in throwing up problems? Much can be learned about the group by the way they interact. A teacher should take every opportunity to observe the class at work.

FROZEN PICTURE

A frozen picture is a very useful strategy for a number of reasons. For one thing it holds up the action of the play and allows the participants to take time to reflect on the significance of events. In constructing a frozen picture the group is invited to crystallize what they see as the important feature of the drama in such a way as to be intelligible to other members of the group.

The instruction to create a frozen picture needs to be carefully worded and the time allowed to construct it needs to be carefully controlled. Experience has shown that a longer length of time does not necessarily produce a 'better' frozen picture. Often a time pressure forces decisions to be made quickly and the instinctive reaction is often in keeping with the real focus of the drama. With time to think and discuss, connections with the original often get blurred. We recommend that for the frozen pictures suggested in this book two minutes is ample preparation time.

Frozen pictures have many uses. For example, if you are dealing with a particularly violent theme, you may wish to avoid representing this in the drama, unless you stylize it. A frozen picture allows the violence to be present but in a safe protected way as it is one frozen moment. A frozen picture is used this way in 'Stabbing at a disco'. Another way that a frozen picture offers protection is shown in 'The story of Maria'. This is a very carefully composed photograph, deliberately chosen to illustrate a particular news story. Maria is not present in the photograph - she is represented by the journalist who is helping the photographer pose exactly the right picture.

The frozen picture used in '1999' is slightly different. The groups have to invent a frozen picture which might have the caption: 'The day in 1999 when everything went wrong for everyone'. In such a picture there may well be more happening than the group have the expertise to represent or the viewer immediately to see. At this point it is useful to introduce the technique where viewers can ask questions of those in the photograph to establish what is being represented.

There are many ways to interrogate a frozen picture and how you organize the questions will depend upon which group you wish to invent the play. Questions focus the picture not only for the watchers but for the participants as well; by answering a question they commit themselves to a particular decision. This may not always be what they had originally had in mind. You can put the watchers in control by allowing them to ask questions which can only be answered yes or no. Insist that the questions be put to the character in the play and not the person. If they do not know the name of the character then they must use something that is immediately recognizable to that character - a piece of clothing or the position they are in. A questioning session might begin:

1   'Girl standing', are you holding something in your hand?
2   'Boy with red jumper', do you know all these people?
3   'Girl lying down', has there been an accident?
4   'Boy standing to one side', are you trying to get away?

In this way the character's clothing or position come to be used as names, and this helps to focus attention on the play rather than on the individuals constructing the picture. Because those in the picture cannot say anything apart from yes or no they can only respond to the questions put. Therefore to a certain extent the viewers are creating the play. Sometimes an answer commits the group to something which means that the next answer must take this into account. In the above example the group may not have considered their scene as an accident, until asked.

Alternatively, you can give the responsibility for explaining the frozen picture to the group that has created it by enabling them to explain the events. One way to do this is through shadowing. As the teacher touches each character on the shoulder they speak one line out loud that their character is thinking. This can be repeated with one line that is actually said in this scene. The frozen picture can be brought to life or moved forward or backward in time.

Obviously you can mix these techniques and have the viewers speak the lines for those in the scene. The important things are that you know why you are using a particular effect and you know what result is likely.

A frozen picture does not have to be a moment selected from the play. It could be the crystallization of how a character is feeling - the symbolic representation of an emotion. This is a very useful way of deepening the response of a group who find it difficult to believe in a particular emotion experienced by one of the characters.

Frozen pictures do not have to be single events. They can form part of a series. In 'The story of Maria' if the newspaper published photographs of Maria taken at different times on the day of her release, these would tell a very clear story. We have called a sequence of frozen pictures cartooning and it is a quick way of detailing a lot of material. For example, at the end of the 'Drugs' structure you could invite the groups to recreate ten frozen pictures that show the points in the drama when one of the dealers made a decision about something. Or you could assemble ten frozen pictures that show the ten different emotions that Maria has felt during her five years in prison. This is an excellent way to review events and can be simply sketched a notebook as a more permanent record.

USE OF STORY

A story is a good way to quickly build a shared context with a group. It could be a story told by the teacher or by the group. It could be something that has been made up by the class or something that someone else has created.

Be aware of the difference between reading, telling, watching and hearing a story. When you read to a class, unless you are very familiar with it, you cannot maintain eye contact with the group. When you tell a story you can engage the group much more directly and illustrate the story with gestures and movement. Stories can be wonderfully embellished with a very few objects.

Children are constantly telling stories, indeed it is one of the ways that they begin to make sense of the world for themselves. Although they may be quite confident about telling stories outside the classroom, inside the classroom with the full glare of an audience upon them may be a different matter. However, you can develop the fluency with which stories are told within a group. Build from simple stories, such as the story of how they came to school today, and then elaborate it by adding details both real and imagined. If everyone is telling a story to a partner then the embarrassment of performing to an audience is removed.

There are many ways that you can use traditional stories and story books in drama. A good way to explore a familiar story is to retell it as one of the characters in the story. The details of a story told by the step mother may be very different to the version told by Cinderella.

It is always interesting to compare the different versions of stories that children have and try to find out where they have come from. Often children remember a story from a pantomime or film. If this is compared with an original story from Grimm or Perrault it is often the more gruesome details that have been left out in the modern versions. Most children have some knowledge of urban myths. Nearly everyone you meet will have a story that begins, 'It didn't happen to me, but a friend of mine told me that ...' These stories can be traced all round the country, often with similar ingredients but with one essential change - all the places mentioned in the story have been localized.

Stories can develop from a picture, photograph or painting. All that is required is that you select a character in the picture to tell the story from their point of view. You could tell the story and ask the class to guess which character is speaking.

Stories are not just a collection of random events or actions. To be successful they must be carefully constructed. Often they reflect a mystical connection in that events often have to occur three times before any change is noticed. Most stories have these things in common:

❏ a who (at least one being)
❏ a location (placing in time is also useful)
❏ a purpose (engine)
❏ a necessity (the need to do it).

You can create stories with a group by asking questions. In this instance it will be important to ask open questions and encourage an imaginative response. It is difficult to ask questions sometimes without leading the response. It is worth working out half a dozen questions in advance that you think open up the story rather than narrow it down. Here are six that we have used, with as little content prescribed as possible, to offer a good start base for group storying:

❏ What was the being like?
❏ Where do such beings live?
❏ Why did this being want to go home?
❏ What was home like?
❏ What might happen if the being didn't get home?
❏ What was the final outcome?

DRAMA RELATED ACTIVITIES

There are occasions when the students are not in role but they need to make decisions about the drama. In `The factory' the whole group contributes to the plan of the factory and then it is `created' in the room.

Often drama related activities happen out of role, but the students could be in role or in a twilight sort of role, half in and half out of the drama. Dorothy Heathcote often works in this way. She frequently interrupts the drama and asks the group to create lists, catalogue objects, look at a map, look at books, create a drawing.

There are times when you may want to gradually edge in to a piece of drama work. At these times you might start by drawing the map of a place or building with the group, as with `The factory', or you might have a jumble of objects and ask, `Who would be the best people to make sense of these?'

Drama related activities support the work and can often allow for a greater depth of meaning to come through by holding up the work for examination, but the activity must be related. It must be something that the characters in the play would actually do. If the students are told to write a story that is one thing; if the police officer is asked to take a statement from the witness that is something completely different.

VIDEO

In schools video is often used poorly. This is possibly due to a belief that because the group are involved with technology they will be absorbed in the process. However, to create a good piece of video which is satisfying for everyone involved takes a long time. Unless everyone has a clear understanding of what part they have to play in the proceedings some will inevitably drop out and get bored.

It may be that you can get the help of the school technician for the period of time that you are using the video camera. If not try to find another adult or older student who has time to assist you. All lessons benefit by having another adult in the room. When using equipment this is almost a necessity. If you have a large number of students to work with then it may be better to organize them into teams and rotate the activities so that they all try a range of activities.

Using a video camera can be very creative. Explore the technical capability of your particular machine. All cameras turn the image as you rotate the camera, so it is easy to create the effect of mountaineers struggling up a steep rock face. By shaking the camera slightly you can make it appear as if there is an earth tremor. Some cameras offer a negative image, which is especially good for any drama work that needs to create mystery or supernatural effects. On most machines you can edit in camera, which means that you can easily create the effect of people disappearing or possessing supernatural powers, like being able to jump on to or off high buildings. It is important that before you use the camera with the group you know how it works and what the potential is. You can then plan accordingly.

You do not need to use the camera just to record practical work in action. You can use it in the play. For example, suppose you are working on the life of a young girl, you could shoot the whole video literally from her point of view. This would include people looking down to talk to her and her looking up to reply and ask questions. Similarly you could do a day in the life of a piece of rubbish or any other object and shoot everything from that imagined perspective. Similarly the camera can become the aggressor and what the viewer sees are images of people running away.

The material that you record can be used in different ways. For example:

- ❑ as evidence
- ❑ as a record of events
- ❑ to give information
- ❑ as proof of something
- ❑ it could become an artefact, or the recording of valuable objects
- ❑ it could belong to someone and be a treasured possession
- ❑ it could be made by one group for one purpose but then taken up by another group for an entirely different reason, as a kind of rolling video drama.

VIDEO

When students watch any piece of video, unless it is purely for fun, they need to have a reason to watch. They could watch in role as detectives to examine a piece of surveillance material. They could watch as customs' officers to see which passengers are acting suspiciously as they wait to be checked through. Or they could watch out of role but primed to pay attention to specific details. For example, notice how flashback is used or make a note of the moments that you feel the suspense is mounting.

The technology of video equipment is something that children are becoming increasingly familiar with. Consequently it is something that deserves attention in our classroom, but it needs to be used creatively.

GAMES

Games are often used as an end in themselves rather than as a valuable way of deepening drama work. Sometimes with a particular group it may be that the only activity you can get them to engage with is a game. In this case the game will fulfil your limited objective. However, there is no point in starting each drama lesson with a series of games in the hope that this prepares the group for the drama. Often it does the opposite by exciting the group to such a pitch that they cannot concentrate.

However, a carefully selected game that leads into the drama work, or one that can support a particular moment in the drama, can be most useful. In 'Waxworks', which is for the most part about the students keeping still and silent, the element of playing a game is important to enhance their motivation towards the activity. In this case the short-term objective of the class, to play the game well, is at odds with the short-term objective of the teacher, which is to improve the ability of the class to create frozen pictures. However, the product is the same. It is important to bring to the attention of the group how they can use their skill from the game in developing their drama work.

Similarly, if in 'Hillside Unit' the inmates were to attempt to escape, a structure that again used 'Grandma's footsteps' might help inject the right feeling of tension. If they have to get across an open courtyard which has a light regularly trained across it and a sentry on patrol the game might help to develop their belief in the situation.

If you examine your own lessons you will find opportunities where the structure of a game could be introduced in order to deepen the response of the group. This is a much more positive use of games than merely playing one after another to fill up time.

USING A MODEL

A model is often useful to set a baseline for the work, especially if you have a group who are reluctant to get straight into the drama. The way we established the model was by working at the front with the others watching. The teacher and volunteers improvised the scene, sometimes spontaneously, sometimes having prepared the work. Then the group was invited to comment on the events and to decide how it could be adapted to improve the quality of the drama.

An example of a scene being modelled to the class appears at the beginning of `Drugs'. The teacher and volunteers act out a scene where two drug dealers attempt to bring drugs in through customs. After the initial portrayal of the scene the group may have their own ideas about how each of the characters should behave in the scene. The original group can try out these ideas or other volunteers can take their place.

The object of the exercise is to create interest in the group for the activity that is taking place. The more they invest in the details of the scene, the more involved they will be with the work. If there is an opportunity for them to experiment in groups their imaginations will already be fired. For those who find drama difficult there is a scene already invented which they can at least copy if they find it difficult to invent beyond it.

RESOURCES

LIST OF RESOURCES

While the lesson structures can be used as they stand there are additional resources provided here which can save preparation time.

Resource 1
A torn note. This could be used in the 'Drugs' structure. It is a careless arrangement to buy drugs. The note could be found in someone's possession, in their belongings, car, or near where they are standing in the street.

Resource 2
An anonymous note scribbled by an inmate at Hillside Unit. If this is found by someone passing by, what is their responsibility? What could happen if the note was given to the media or police? What if the person took the note to show the warden? Or if the warden was that passer by?

Resource 3
A letter for 'The story of Maria'. A letter to Maria from her mother which is received shortly before she gets out of prison. This extra information could be obtained by the journalists at any stage. The group must try to decide what it all means.

Resource 4
Headline for 'Hillside Unit' structure. This could be used as a stimulus.

Resource 5
Customs declaration poster for use with the 'Drugs' structure. Going through the details on the list and having the smugglers answer 'no' as each question is asked will help to add tension to this static opening scene.

Resource 6
The poster announcing the disco which occurs in the structure 'Stabbing at a Disco'. The head of year could wave this poster at the assembly to show that this is what all the fuss is about.

Resource 7
The rules for the inmates of Hillside Unit. The warden could go through these when the new inmates arrive. Alternatively the group could prepare their own set of rules.

Resource 8
A blank statement form. This could be used in the 'Interrogation' structure. Eventually the paper is signed by the character under pressure but remains blank.

What does the character confess to or what do his / her interrogators write on the paper and accuse him / her of?

Resource 9

Health and Safety notice for 'The Factory' structure. If this is displayed throughout the drama the management could claim that they have fulfilled their legal responsibility. But is this sufficient?

Resource 10

Poster welcoming people to Time Travel Inc. friendly, but with a hint of something being not quite right. This could be used to establish the situation in the structure 'Time Travel Inc.' where the teacher in role welcomes the travellers. It may also bring in the extra concept of humankind's responsibility to nature. Animals are disappearing due to human greed, pollution and over farming. The only way to see some species now is to travel back in time.

Resource 11

Agenda for the year council meeting in 'Stabbing at a disco'. Remember the head has organized the agenda deliberately to exclude discussion of the disco. If the group wish to raise this it must come under AOB, but there will be a time pressure as the meeting cannot run beyond the lunch hour (or whatever deadline is set). As well as adding to the drama this sheet could be used to help to explain how meetings are organized.

Resource 12

An old, well-used map, which is the route to a plantation where drugs are being grown. This can become the stimulus for part of the development work in the structure 'Drugs'. The group find the producer of the drugs, but he / she is just a peasant farmer. What should they do now? If they tell the police the farmer will lose his livelihood and the family will starve. If they do nothing the drugs will continue to be sold. What conversation do they have with the farmer?

Resource 13

Drawing of ten boxes each with different objects inside - large spider, money, jewellery, books and diaries, snake, monkey, another smaller box, a map, an old fob watch with an inscription that can't quite be read, war medals. This drawing can be used to support the work being developed in 'The box'. Students can, of course, invent for themselves what is in the box when it comes to the pairs exercise, but it may be useful to have some starter ideas. Also, by restricting the number of possibilities and allocating specific objects to specific groups positive critical observation can be encouraged by asking those watching the mime to suggest which object is being reacted to. This can then develop into a session to refine presentation skills.

Resource 14
Storyboard outline for use with `Making a video drama'. One box to be completed for each shot that needs to be taken.

Resource 15
A blank **Advanced Organizer** for you to use to devise your own lesson plans.

Resource 16
Press card and press photographer's pass, to be used by journalists who are attempting to find Maria (or by any journalists in a different drama). They should help to reinforce the idea that the journalists could lose their jobs and have their press cards taken away if it becomes of symbolic importance in the drama.

Photographs and Pictures
Photographs and pictures are always a good way of starting off a drama lesson. These three are included here to support structures contained in this book, but each could be used in alternative ways. Remember, the photograph itself could become an object in the drama. It could be something someone hides, finds, steals or destroys. It could be used as evidence against someone, or for blackmail. With some imagination a photograph can conjure up interesting opportunities for drama, but it needs the skill which the teacher provides to grasp them and bring them to life.

Resource 17
Photograph of a young woman standing outside a forbidding prison as if she is just leaving. This could be used in `The story of Maria' by the editor. He / she could show it to the journalists as he / she tells the story.

Resource 18
Picture of a collection of waxworks. This could be used as a prop by the storyteller who could tell the frightening story about the waxworks and then say something like, `... and I had a nightmare about the place the other night. I woke up three times in a cold sweat. In the morning I was still shaking. And do you know what I found when I was making the bed? ... This! (shows picture) Now how do you explain that?'

Resource 19
Picture of a futuristic landscape - with objects which could possibly be dwellings. This could be used in the development work for `1999'. When the people arrive on the new planet this is what they see. The unfamiliar aspect makes them all miss `home'. While waiting to be placed in the Rehabilitation Centre they could tell each other stories of the `good times' back on Earth. These stories could be acted out in a sequence of flashbacks.

Resource 1

IF YOU WANT SOME MORE OF THE SAME —
SAME PLACE, SAME TIME.
BRING PLENTY OF MONEY.

Resource 2

To whoever finds this note

I'm writing this from the Hillside Unit. You've no idea what it's like here. We're supposed to be here 'cause we've done something wrong, but we haven't, leastways nobody's ever told me. It's like a prison. We're hardly allowed out and worst of all some of my friends have disappeared.

If you find this note please give it to the newspapers.

Resource 3

23 Dryden Road,
Islington
N1
15 March 1991

Dear Maria,

It seems like ages since I last visited. I was so sad to see you so depressed. I know you set your heart on being released at Christmas but the Governor said he could not turn a blind eye — or at least a black one.

It's not like you to be in a fight. Why won't you tell me what she said? I suppose it must have been something personal.

I talked with our solicitor. He says there is no way you'll have to serve the full seven years. It's nearly five now — still you know that. You'll soon be home.

The garden's beginning to look good again. A mild winter always brings the flowers on. The bulbs are really something special this year and the daffodils! Your dad would have liked them.

Write and let me know if there is anything you need. I'll visit you again soon. Oh, and the solicitor says I should tell you [CENSORED, CENSORED] so keep up hope.

All my love,
Mum XXX.

The Sentinal

FRIDAY JULY 6TH 1992   **40P**

DRAMA GROUP SENT TO SECURE UNIT

Do You Have Anything To Declare?

British Nationals returning from Europe are allowed the following with no extra duty to pay:

| 200 Cigarettes | 2 Litres of Still Table Wine | 1 Litre of Spirits | 60cc of perfume | £32 worth of Gifts, Souvenirs and other goods. |

If this applies to you proceed through the green lanes marked 'Nothing to Declare'.

If however you have excess of the above or other items to declare move immediately to the red lanes.

Government Warning: Anyone attempting to avoid paying the appropriate duty will be prosecuted.

HM CUSTOMS

The Insiders
Youth Club

Proudly present

the loudest... coolest... hottest...

Disco

**in the history of
the universe**

**Tonight at the Youth Centre
from 8 till late...**

Hillside Unit

Rules

1) Inmates to answer politely when spoken to and show respect for warders at all times. When addressing a warder use `Sir' or `Madam'.

2) Inmates will take all meals in the communal dinning area and take responsibility for collecting meals and clearing away. Washing up will be done on a rota system.

3) Inmates will be required to keep their room clean and tidy at all times. Any room found untidy at the time of either a routine inspection or an emergency inspection will cause that inmate loss of privileges.

4) Landings and all floor areas to be washed and disinfected every day. A rota will be in operation. Inmates to check the noticeboard each morning and take responsibility for their shift. Anyone failing to complete their shift will immediately lose all privileges for one week.

5) All not on a work detail should report to the education office each day at 08.00 and 12.45.

6) Recreational period is from 16.00 to 18.00. The library is open during this period.

7) Lights will be turned out at 21.00.

8) Smoking is not permitted.

9) Inmates are permitted one visit per month.

10) Inmates who have any complaint about conditions must make an appointment to see the Warden.

By order HM Government.

Interrogation Unit

STATEMENT MADE BY _____

SIGNED _____

DATE _____

Health and Safety at Work Act 1974

Your employer has a duty under the law to ensure, so far as is reasonably practicable, your health, safety and welfare at work.

In general, your employer's duties include:

■ **Making your workplace safe and without risks to health;**

■ **Keeping dust, fume and noise under control;**

■ **Ensuring plant and machinery are safe and that safe systems of work are set and followed;**

■ **Ensuring articles and substances are moved, stored and used safely;**

■ **Providing adequate welfare facilities;**

■ **Giving you the information, instruction, training and supervision necessary for your health and safety.**

Welcome to

Time Travel Inc.

The company that put time travel on the map.

Rest assured that we will deliver you safely to your destination of choice and return you safely.

Please feel free to examine our trophy room. All the exhibits are genuine copies of animals which actually existed on our earth in the past.

If you see any time zone you would care to visit do talk with one of our friendly assistants seated at one of the terminals at the service desk.

Remember our motto:

your past is safe in our hands.

**Thank you for your interest in
Time Travel Inc.**

Agenda for the Year Council Meeting on

1)	Apologies

2)	Minutes from last meeting

3)	Matters arising

4)	Removal of school uniform for Sixth Year

5)	Fifth Year end of exams outing

6)	Lower school sports day

7)	AOB

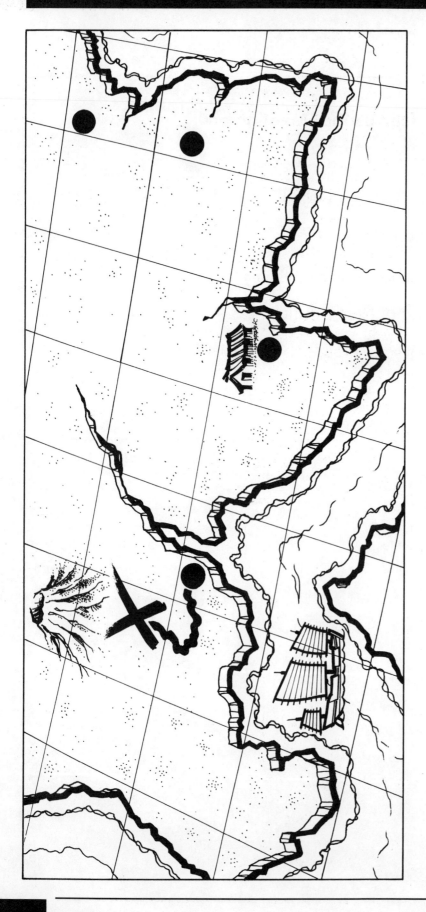

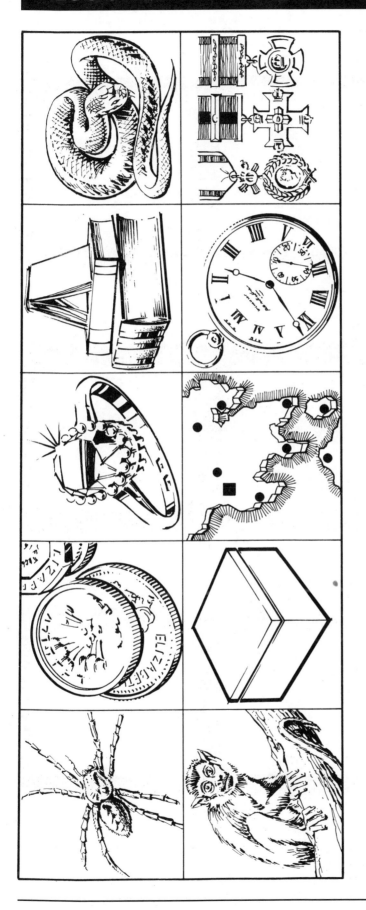

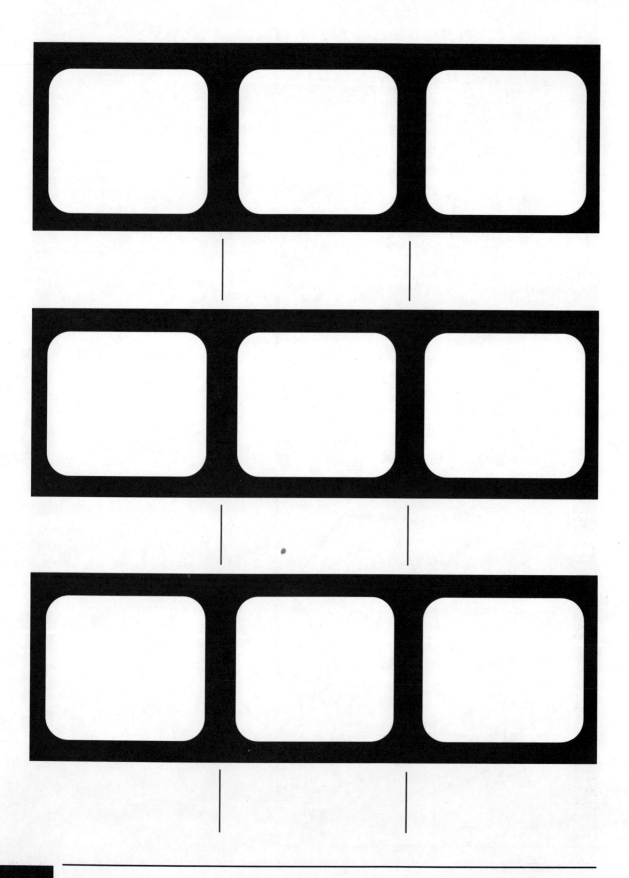

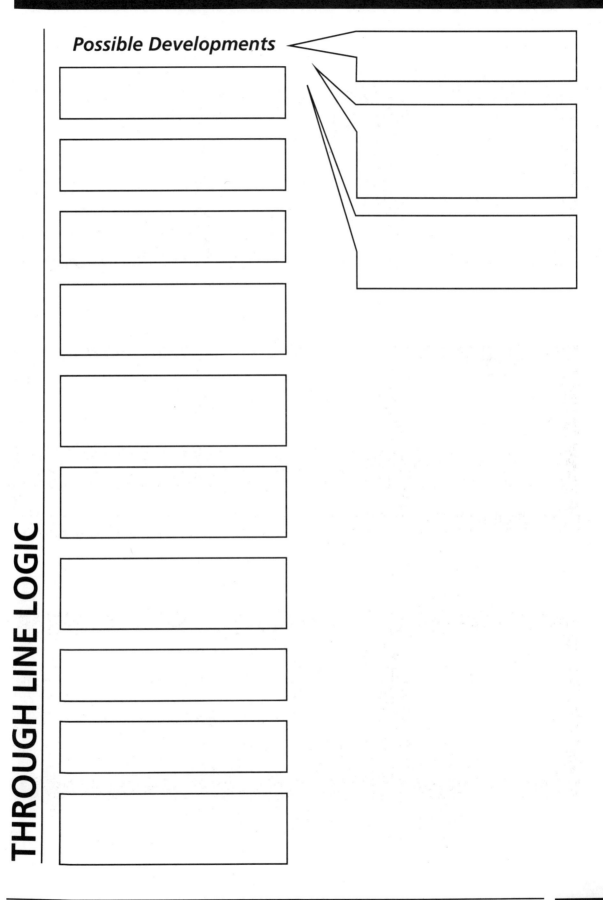

Possible Developments

THROUGH LINE LOGIC

PRESS

NAME: *John Smith*

PUBLICATION: *The Sentinal*

JOB TITLE: *Journalist*

NUJ NUMBER: *44 5678 122*

DATE OF ISSUE: *04/07/1991*

AUTHORISED

P.F.Hunter

PRESS

NAME: *Sue Parker*

PUBLICATION: *The Sentinal*

JOB TITLE: *Photographer*

NUJ NUMBER: *44 5678 122*

DATE OF ISSUE: *04/07/1991*

AUTHORISED

P.F.Hunter

RESOURCE 17 - PHOTOGRAPHS AND PICTURES

Resource 18

Resource 19